Soul Traders

How honest people lost out to hard sell

Jonathan Gabay

Marshall Cavendish
Business

For all those I have taught and those from whom I am yet to learn.

With thanks to Martin Liu, Maurice Benzimra, Catherine Burch, David Abbott, Pom Somkabcharti, the Faculty of the Chartered Institute of Marketing and the twin sources of the sincerest nectar for my soul—Michelle and Joshua.

Copyright © 2009 Jonathan Gabay

First published in 2009 by:

Marshall Cavendish Limited
Fifth Floor
32–38 Saffron Hill
London EC1N 8FH
United Kingdom
T: +44 (0)20 7421 8120
F: +44 (0)20 7421 8121
sales@marshallcavendish.co.uk
www.marshallcavendish.co.uk

Marshall Cavendish is a trademark of Times Publishing Limited

Other Marshall Cavendish offices:
Marshall Cavendish International (Asia) Private Limited, 1 New Industrial Road, Singapore 536196 • Marshall Cavendish Corporation. 99 White Plains Road, Tarrytown NY 10591-9001, USA • Marshall Cavendish International (Thailand) Co Ltd. 253 Asoke, 12th Floor, Sukhumvit 21 Road, Klongtoey Nua, Wattana, Bangkok 10110, Thailand • Marshall Cavendish (Malaysia) Sdn Bhd, Times Subang, Lot 46, Subang Hi-Tech Industrial Park, Batu Tiga, 40000 Shah Alam, Selangor Darul Ehsan, Malaysia

The right of Jonathan Gabay to be identified as the author of this work has been asserted by him in accordance with the Copyright, Designs and Patents Act 1988.

A CIP record for this book is available from the British Library

ISBN 978-1-905736-51-5

Designed and typeset by Cambridge Publishing Management Ltd

Printed and bound in Great Britain by MPG Books Ltd, Bodmin, Cornwall

Contents

A season is set for everything, a time for every experience
under heaven;
A time for being born and a time for dying,
A time for planting and a time for uprooting the planted;
A time for slaying and a time for healing,
A time for tearing down and a time for building up;
A time for weeping and a time for laughing,
A time for wailing and a time for dancing;
A time for throwing stones and a time for gathering stones,
A time for embracing and a time for shunning embraces;
A time for seeking and a time for losing,
A time for keeping and a time for discarding;
A time for ripping and a time for sewing,
A time for silence and a time for speaking;
A time for loving and a time for hating;
A time for war and a time for peace.

Ecclesiastes 3:1–8, JPS Tanakh

Preface

Recently I heard something that shocked me. I was delivering a two-day European Web 2.0 marketing event to senior communications figures working in commerce, science, and politics.

Over lunch, a German delegate said he knew of a very successful company that could arrange for thousands of protestors to carry placards displaying any message. The crowd would happily remonstrate—with fervor and passion about a chosen subject—be it political or commercial—as long as they were paid in advance. I was shaken by what he said.

Over 30 years I have proudly been involved in all aspects of creative marketing and communications, and worked for many major brands' international advertisers and PR agencies. I have taught literally thousands of enthusiastic marketers around the world how sincere and well-practiced marketing can add value to them and their customers by building businesses, confidence and causes. Over the decades marketing has inspired, informed and helped many people achieve their goals. However, while many brand leaders show us the way forward, some practitioners have long operated from a very different rule book.

Rather than aspire to the best business practices, some marketing professionals and media have either knowingly or inadvertently morphed into a parasitic force. I call this group the soul traders. It's a group that is often brilliant in its execution. Ultimately, though, it sadly leads the public to view marketing professionals with distrust.

This book explores the carefully manicured stories that spin out from generation after generation of this less-than-honorable variety of marketing specialists. Thanks to the power of such practitioners, even long-established and previously reputable banks, entrusted as custodians of people's money, have lost their way. Now we see those institutions exposed as greedy parasites.

In 2008, the day before Lehman Brothers filed for bankruptcy, the conspiracy theorist Donald Luskin was quoted by the *Washington Post* as saying, "Anyone who says we're in a recession, or heading into one—especially the worst one since the Great Depression—is making up his own private definition of 'recession'." On Christmas Day in the same year, the leader of the Roman Catholic Church in England and Wales blamed the credit crunch for a "breakdown" in social trust.

With the help of marketing hype, the biggest flimflam in decades had successfully convinced working-class people to invest in a product whose very name suggested it wasn't exactly the best in the market: "sub-prime mortgages." The fallout from the sting left bankers asking just about anyone to spare them a dime, penny, or any currency with value still left. Just four months after the collapse of Lehman Brothers *et al*, Reuters reported an American 26-year high in the number of jobless people filing for benefits. At the start of 2009, the UK Chartered Institute of Personnel and Development predicted at least 600,000 jobs would be lost within a year. Even small businesses relying on honest marketing to sell their wares and services were expected to fold at the rate of over 185 a day.

> *They say the next big thing is here,*
> *that the revolution's near,*
> *but to me it seems quite clear*
> *that it's all just a little bit of history repeating*
>
> Alex Gifford, Propellerheads, "History Repeating"

This erosion of trust isn't solely down to the credit crisis of the late 2000s. Its roots go deep into the history of the soul traders. Many students, journalists and associates urged me to address the commercial and political history leading to the current state of the industry openly and honestly. Many organizations would have preferred me not to have written this book at all as it reveals a side of the business which until now—officially at least—has been at best glossed over, and at worst, ignored.

I prefer openness. Truly great marketing has always touched people because of its integrity and honesty. The days of sticking heads in the sand hoping for a storm to pass simply because of brand vanity and pompous arrogance are over. Capitalism has changed. Rather than be frivolous, society is urged to be frugal with both money and energy. Consequently, society is in danger of becoming bereft of hope. It's time for a marketing reformation that challenges assumptions and restores faith and confidence.

As in war, the first casualty of soul-trader-led marketing is truth. As you will read, this is nothing new. The real scandal is that casualties are still hobbling in from the battlefield, bloodied and wretched—despite history's lessons and warnings. All too often politicians switch from being butterflies of hope to grubby spin doctors. They concoct bogus promises driven through with fake authenticity and ultimately leave voters strung out on a cocktail of confusion and bewilderment. Hard-pressed journalists report increasingly short summaries rather than offer in-depth coverage. They have been forced to become wind socks changing direction according to PR spin emailed over from parties offering the gloomiest, most startling or harrowing version of a story. Viewers, listeners and bloggers are left with so many divided opinions that the background to facts becomes hidden in the immediacy of a suitably sensation-grabbing new opinion, forming a fleeting consensus until the next news bulletin is released.

The same is true in commerce, which is supposed to be driven by competitive choice. Rather than being helped to enjoy their choices, consumers are abandoned, and left to trudge through a pungent swamp of blandness, bordered by endless streams of me-too politically correct products, TV shows, movies, political promises and "must-have" services.

The influence of spin doctors over choice has become so powerful that in the name of political correctness, the UK's

Channel Four broadcast an official New Year message to the people of Britain delivered by one of the biggest threats to peace in the world: the President of Iran—Mahmoud Ahmadinejad.

It was a prime example of a phenomenon described at the time by the *Guardian* newspaper as "double-hyping," where celebrities and their critics share an interest in exaggerating the celebrity's importance even if that importance has no substance. The soul traders were at work again.

We have reached a "tipping point." Consumers, voters, viewers, followers, all are growing increasingly sensitive to carefully manicured messages adorned with plastic sincerity. Blanket bombed with messages headlined by the word "believe," they have come to recognize the hidden reality of "be*lie*ve." People have become numb to border conflicts and wars in far-flung fields and battles on high streets.

Equally despondent are well-intentioned professionals managing brands, images and causes. Rather than use their hard-won skills and talents, many have been reduced to seeking out efficiencies for streamlining the production of products and services to be delivered to as many people in the shortest time at the cheapest price. Such products and services provide the perception, not the reality of quality.

The only social group left to excel, appear to be parrot-programmed accountants equipped to judge creativity through the windows of a spreadsheet or institutionalized paper pushers preoccupied with political games, rather than reaching out to the ordinary man or woman in the street.

Erstwhile creative communication thinkers, increasingly threatened by the fear of not complying to standardized corporate escape clauses and brand guidelines, are pressurized to produce more and more messages in less and less time, for an audience suffering from A.D.D. (Advertising Deluge Disorder). Marketers, PR professionals, copywriters, designers, sponsors, media agents, sales and brand managers have all become like factory-line workers, dependent on "cut and paste" rather than being encouraged to exercise their creativity. Is it any wonder so many enthusiastic communication professionals end up as cynics?

It is time for a change. You can sense it everywhere.

Not just political change, as promised by President Obama who swept into office with a landslide snoot at the old establishment. Nor just a commercial change as espoused by manufacturers of increasingly diminutive phones and computers featuring progressively thicker chunks of memory. Not even a radical change as preached to directionless zealots prepared to sacrifice their lives in the vain hope of leaving a message of purpose.

A judiciously principled marketing reformation challenges long-held assumptions. This book considers all our yesterdays in order to learn from them, and to have some kind of ethically sensible and commercially sustainable tomorrow.

Don't be mistaken. This book is not a protest on behalf of the latest trend. Neither is it a rant about crackpot conspiracies. In my experience most conspiracies turn out to be vacuous vessels rather than gunpowder plots. I am not really the sort of person who believes in UFOs or stands on the kerb shaking my fist at every passing vehicle of greed, power and excess that speeds by.

This quest for understanding is based on the premise that the search is essential if we are to uncover the truth. Voyages of exploration form the foundation of any lesson in business ethics and marketing reformation. Unconfined by geographical borders and open to debate, here is the real unexpurgated story of marketing and propaganda's rise and fall . . . and . . . well, I'll leave it to you to turn the pages of understanding to discover for yourself.

Jonathan Gabay
www.soultraderstruth.com

Introduction:
Your journey begins

I am going to take you to high and far-flung corners of the world, backwards and forwards in time. Walking past the neon glare of advertising billboards you'll explore seldom-trodden side alleys, leading to the deepest, darkest parts of commercial marketing, social science and political propaganda. You'll discover pathways that link future mistakes to the present promises and past propaganda.

I am going to show you the whole truth in all its shades and hues.

Our journey starts halfway up a limestone cliff linking the ancient Iranian cities of Babylonia and Media. Here there is a tremendous inscription measuring 15 meters high and 25 meters long. Carved by hand, it depicts a bearded Darius I of Persia. His left foot bears down on the chest of a man who foolishly tried to overthrow the monarchy. Two servants surround Darius and ten subjects, representing nations conquered by Darius, are bound by hand and neck. Gazing up at the impressive inscribed slab one feels a sense of awe, many centuries after it was first inscribed around 460 BCE. It is one of the few surviving examples of the world's first marketing propaganda—not selling products or services, but allegiance, trepidation and deference to the power-brand of royalty.

Some 600 years and 3,400 kilometers away, a man in a brightly-lit room studies the gilded icon standing on a table. The piece belongs to an organization demanding nothing less than the total redemption of people's souls: the Catholic Church. In our next destination, you'll learn how the labyrinthine development of propagating religious faith would eventually become associated with a wider political and commercial ambition for control and power.

1

The brand of Church and empire

Now the serpent was more crafty than any other beast of the field that the Lord God had made . . .

Genesis 3:1

The church of consumerism and political ministry of authority had their foundations in quite a different belief system altogether. Their main objective was to spread a specific message of authority and might to all people —although in some cases some of those people were more "equal" than others.

Churches were among the first institutions to use marketing to sell themselves internationally and to use what might now be thought of as propaganda to convey their message. Martin Luther (1483–1546) was one of the first to use propaganda to convey a religiously biased message. Luther challenged the papacy by arguing that the only source of religious authority lay with the Bible itself rather than with any church official. He published posters depicting the Pope as the Anti-Christ as well as a book called *On the Jews and their Lies* (1543). Centuries later the book would be cited by the Nazis in their own propaganda as justification to slaughter six million Jews.

The early seventeenth century marked the closing stages of the Age of Discovery that had started back in the fifteenth century. Each newly discovered land had offered religions such as Islam and Christianity greater opportunity to spread their teachings through missionary work. But as the hope of discovering more uncharted lands quickly diminished, the Roman Catholic Church was increasingly concerned about how to extend its teachings to the natives in the discovered world. It didn't want to lose its worldwide grip on people.

Pope Gregory XIII (1572–85) felt duty-bound to evangelize in countries such as England and Holland where Protestantism was spreading rapidly. Under Gregory, the Holy See's struggle to achieve such a goal would eventually lead to the establishment of the Sacred Congregation of Propaganda. The word "propaganda" was chosen because its Latin stem *propagand* conveyed a sense of "that which ought to be spread."

The propaganda plan was put into action and a commission recommended the foundation of foreign seminaries along with the printing of catechisms and similar works in many languages. But within seven years of Gregory XIII's death the commission's work ground to a virtual stop. While the commission members died off, the pressure to respond to growing numbers of Protestants and non-Christians did not ease. Enter Pope Gregory XV (1621–3), who established a permanent congregation for the propagation of Catholicism. On June 22, 1622, the Sacred Congregation "de Propaganda Fide" (the sacred Congregation for the Propagation of the Faith) was instituted, with palatial headquarters constructed near the Spanish Steps in Rome. Nearby a street today is still known as Via di Propaganda.

Over the years, the business of the propagating or "marketing" of Catholicism continued. In order to reach different people, for centuries the Congregation's Polyglot printing press published liturgies and catechisms in a multitude of alphabets, including one of the first European books published in Japanese.

Other nations use "force"; we Britons alone use "Might."

Novelist Evelyn Waugh, on the British attitude to imperial conquest

Fast-forward to 1899 and the sun-kissed shores of what is by now one of the fully established outposts of another propagator of its way of life—the British Empire. In places such as East Africa, British culture was marketed in very much the same way as products back in the motherland, with conceit and contempt for "uncivilized" outsiders' and unsubstantiated claims.

For example, back home products such as "Vigor's Horse-Action Saddle," which echoed a sense of the military, were advertised with copy promising:

"The readiest road to health is by means of physical exercise, and the easiest and readiest mode of exercise is by using Vigor's Horse-Action Saddle—which not only provides, as Dr George Fleming, C.C., writes: 'A Perfect Substitute for the Live Horse but acts so beneficially upon the system as to be of almost priceless value. It promotes good spirits, quickens the circulation, stimulates the liver, reduces corpulence, creates appetite, cures indigestion and gout.'"

Meanwhile other brands such as Pears' Soap were using largely unregulated advertising to promote the British Empire's missionary zeal to educate the savage colonies into understanding the ethics of the West. One advertisement for Pears' Soap played on the trials of the West to civilize native outsiders so they could become enlightened and fulfilled through serving the needs of the sophisticated well-to-do and gentry in both America and Britain.

"The first step towards lightening the white man's burden is through teaching the virtues of cleanliness. Pears' Soap is a potent factor in brightening the dark corners of the earth as civilization advances, while amongst the cultured of all nations it holds the highest place—it is the ideal toilet soap."

The advertisement from 1899 featured George Dewey, an impeccably well-dressed American Navy admiral. Dewey, dressed in a smart white uniform, was pictured washing his hands in an electrically-lit cabin as his steamship sailed towards the edges of the British Empire. The advertisement's central scene is framed with views showing a fleet sailing towards new territories, as well as a picture of an unkempt black native African kneeling at the feet of a white trader. The native gratefully accepts a bar of soap from the benevolent trader.

At the time a white supremacist race-marketing theme was internationally commonplace. A 1916 magazine advert, copyrighted by Morris & Bendien, showed a black child drinking ink. The caption read, "Nigger Milk." A year earlier in 1915, American D. W. Griffith directed what was to become considered by many movie historians as one of the most influential movies of all time: *Birth of a Nation*. It appealed to class prejudices, and it also explored sinister social undercurrents of racism. Its biased, sympathetic and highly controversial account of the rise of the racist Ku Klux Klan (KKK) encouraged some moviegoers from the American South to put on white masks and join the KKK, making it the world's first recruitment movie for a cause—albeit a terrible one.

Everyday household items including toys, postcards, ashtrays, detergent boxes, fishing lures, and children's books frequently portrayed black people with swollen eyes, oversized lips, and jet-black skin, and either naked or poorly clothed. In 1874, the McLoughlin Brothers of New York marketed a puzzle game called "Chopped Up Niggers." From 1878, the B. Leidersdorf Company of Milwaukee, Wisconsin, produced "NiggerHair Smoking Tobacco." In 1917, the American Tobacco Company had a "NiggerHair" redemption promotion. "NiggerHair" coupons were redeemable for "cash, tobacco, S. & H. Green stamps, or presents."

Fortunately with the advent of more liberal thinking at the beginning of the twentieth century, bigoted, narrow-minded upper-class attitudes began to wane. The time was long overdue for a more inclusive approach toward addressing the marketplace. Rather than simply pamper to the privileged elite, a new strategy would be implemented to capture the imagination and support of the general public as a whole. A commercial coup d'état over consumer control was to take place, underpinned by sophisticated propaganda ideals that wouldn't just spread to far-flung colonies but change perceptions of all classes and sexes living, working and praying at the core of the market itself.

2

The engineering
of consent

*Whatever of social importance is done
today, whether in politics, finance,
manufacture, agriculture, charity,
education, or other fields, must be done
with the help of propaganda. Propaganda
is the executive arm of the invisible
government.*

Edward Bernays, *Propaganda*, 1928

The period around World War I was a turning point in the history of political manipulation. The American government wanted to protect its trade and to do so it needed to join in the war. From this emerged a need to "sell" the war to the American people in order to get their support for joining the bloody struggle in Europe. New ideas in psychology led to new ambitions to manipulate public consent, headed up by a man called Edward Bernays. One of his campaigns, lighting the torch of liberty, ignited a revolution that would change the demographics of consumerism forever.

In 1914 Edward Bernays, a bright 23-year-old Viennese press agent, had big plans to alter people's perception of happiness. His strategies were so immense and his tactics so incisive that they would eventually reshape modern marketing.

Bernays was the double-nephew of Sigmund Freud (his mother was Freud's sister; his father was Freud's wife's brother). During visits to his uncle Sigmund in the Swiss Alps, Bernays slowly formulated groundbreaking ideas on how to merge theories of mass psychology with techniques to help commercial and political corporate bodies persuade customers and the electorate alike to follow "party lines."

With the outbreak of the World War I, Bernays' ideas caught the imagination of a devout Presbyterian who, in addition to following a creed of strictly observed order and formality, also just happened to be the 28th President of America: Thomas Woodrow Wilson.

On April 13, 1917, the Committee on Public Information, also known as the CPI and the Creel Committee, was established. It was headed by an investigative journalist called George Creel. Through a heady cocktail of advertising, public relations and general propaganda, the committee's aim was to sway public opinion towards supporting America's intervention in the war. This was essential because whilst Wilson publicly asserted America's fight to "make the world safe for democracy," privately the presidential ambassador to Britain, W. H. Page, explained that declaring war on Germany was, "the only way of maintaining our present pre-eminent trade status."

Notable amongst key Creel committee members was Carl Robert Byoir, who went on to found the world's largest public relations firms in the 1930s. Other committee members included Walter Lippmann,a Harvard language and philosophy major from New York. Like Creel, Lipmann was a journalist with a disdain for liberal communism. The other central committee member was Bernays, who said, "the essence of democratic society" was the "engineering of consent."

Initially the CPI set out to explain their cause by showing hard facts, with a positive twist (or "spin") to support a message of "bringing democracy to all Europe." But before long the committee's spin lost momentum. To turn facts to potent use, the CPI turned to the emerging movie industry. Hollywood scriptwriters were commissioned to produce short but fear-provoking movies. One example was *The Claws of the Hun*, which told the story of John Stanton, the son of munitions magnate Godfrey Stanton, unfairly labeled as a draftdodger In the movie John redeems himself when he discovers German espionage agents attempting to sabotage his father's munitions plant. Another movie, *The Beast of Berlin*, exposed the "wicked" Kaiser's intimate life. In *To Hell with The Kaiser*, the Kaiser, and the Crown Prince are both ridiculed by a brave American girl and several American prisoners of war.

Hollywood plots like these were supported by propaganda, including leaflets warning the American people to be wary of German spies driven by a Germanic blood lust to skewer innocent babies on bayonets. And of course, one of the most memorable slogans created by Creel was "The war to end all wars."

Just in case the general public didn't catch the movies or buy newspapers, Creel also created the Division of Pictorial Publicity. This featured the artwork of artists including Charles Dana Gibson, Louis D. Fancher, and arguably the best-remembered of all—James Montgomery Flagg. It was Flagg who created the now-iconic image of Uncle Sam urging young men to enlist into the army. Over four million posters of Uncle Sam pointing directly out of the poster were printed between 1917 and 1918 and reprinted during World War II.

The Americans weren't alone in producing movie propaganda. Lenin also used cinema to entertain and educate the masses. Movies like *Photomontage* depicted an ideal world. And in the 1920s, three years after the Russian Revolution, the Soviet director Sergei Eisenstein produced movies such as *Strike*, *October* and *Battleship Potemkin*, which highlighted class conflict.

Campaigns such as the "Uncle Sam" project encouraged the establishment of the American Association of Advertising Agencies (1918). By today's standards they would be considered elitist rather than inclusive, with the first president of the Association, for example, describing the use of the word "ad" instead of "advertising" as "the language of bootblacks . . . beneath the dignity of men of the advertising profession."

Uncle Sam's family tree

The story behind Uncle Sam is remarkable. The poster was based on an advertisement from Britain showing Lord Kitchener. But in addition to Lord Kitchener's influence, the Uncle Sam character owed much of its heritage to the Revolutionary War cartoon characters, Brother Jonathan and Yankee Doodle.

Many believe there really was an Uncle Sam. The name was associated with a businessman from Troy, N.Y., Samuel Wilson, known as "Uncle Sam" Wilson. Wilson supplied crates of beef to the army during the war of 1812. The crates were branded "U.S." This could have meant either U.S. property or "Uncle Sam." This branding led to the widespread use of the nickname "Uncle Sam" for the United States. A resolution passed by Congress on September 15, 1961 recognized Wilson as the namesake of the national symbol.

The men of the minute

Fast-forward to the era of the Creel Committee. Driven by public frenzy, service departments suddenly cropped up everywhere. Organizations included the Anti-German Empire Movement and American Protective League, which at its height of popularity claimed to have 250,000 members throughout 600 American cities. The Attorney General, Thomas Gregory, appointed by the Wilson administration, overlooked many of APL's nefarious activities, including alleged beatings, telephone tappings, and making German-Americans kiss the Stars and Stripes flag.

A force of 75,000 politically-primed propaganda enthusiasts called the "Four Minute Men" worked in over 5,000 communities delivering short but passionate talks at public meetings. Records show that a typical speech would include rhetoric such as:

> "Either we shall walk down the Kaiser's streets or his soldiers will goose-step along Pennsylvania Avenue. The sons of liberty (the 'Four Minute Men') are here to defend our great nation."

In 1919, with the war over, the CPI was abolished. That left intellectual powerhouses like Bernays with time on their hands. But not for long. Bernays said:

"I decided that if you could use propaganda for war, you could use if for peace. 'Propaganda' was a bad word because the Germans used it. So what I did was to try to find some other words such as 'Council for Public Relations'."

Edward Bernays, *Propaganda*

Moving out of the CPI and setting up shop in a Broadway office with his future wife, Doris Fleischman, Bernays became the world's first public relations counsellor. His reputation was boosted by publishing a worthy tome espousing his theories that:

"If we understand the mechanism and motives of the group mind . . . it is possible to control and regiment the masses according to our will without their knowing about it."

In 1923, he delivered the world's first PR course at the University of New York—although some claim his competitor, Ivy Ledbetter Lee, held this particular accolade. In 1927, John Wiley Hill opened his public relations company which eventually went on to prosper as the world's largest PR communications companies: Hill & Knowlton.

Back in Vienna, Uncle Sigmund continued to send Bernays books on psychoanalysis. Bernays also read the works of a British neurosurgeon called Wilfred Trotter, who coined the concept of Herd Behaviour. This described how individuals in a group acted together without planned direction. Trotter explained that although during moments of crisis (for example, street demonstrations, football riots, episodes of mob violence) crowds appeared to act as a unit, in reality they were controlled by the uncoordinated behavior of self-seeking individuals.

Whilst visiting Paris, Bernays came across the works of Gustave Le Bon. Drawing on the ideas of Jean-Gabriel de Tarde, in his book *Psychologie des foules* (1895), Le Bon had argued that "in a crowd the conscious personality of an individual was naturally submissive, dominated instead by a collective crowd mind that was unanimous, emotional and intellectually weak." This idea fascinated Bernays. He set out to discover if such theories could be used commercially for corporate America. One of his first clients was George Washington Hill, president of the American Tobacco Company (ATC). Hill was driven by one thing alone—sales.

At the time smoking was big business and essentially the preserve of men. The few women brazen enough to smoke in public were considered to be *femmes fatales*. This view of women who smoked was typified years earlier, in the city of Boston. In 1851, an Irish-born American called Lola Montez had her photograph taken in a studio. In the photograph Montez held a limp cigarette in her black-gloved hand. In the nineteenth century this was considered to be extremely saucy.

Appreciating that Hill was losing half of his potential clients— women—Bernays visited A. A. Brill, a friend and psychologist based in New York. Brill was also an admirer of Freud's theories. Discussing Bernays' new client, ATC, Brill suggested that in his opinion the real reason women didn't smoke was that subconsciously women associated cigarettes with a phallus, representing male sexual power. Brill noted:

> "Some women regard cigarettes as symbols of freedom . . . Smoking is a sublimation of oral eroticism; holding a cigarette in the mouth excites the oral zone. It is perfectly normal for women to want to smoke cigarettes. Further the first women who smoked probably had an excess of male components and adopted the habit as a masculine act. But today the emancipation of women has suppressed many feminine desires. More women now do the same work as men do . . . Cigarettes, which are equated with men, become torches of freedom."
>
> Edward Bernays, *The Engineering of Consent*

Brill suggested that Bernays should challenge this power on behalf of women, so they could erect their own icon of power. The "torches of freedom" concept rang bells in Bernays' mind. All he had to do was find the right time and place to send out his PR message to the world.

As it happened, the city of New York was preparing for the traditional Easter Parade. This had captured the American public's imagination since the 1870s. At the time the Easter Parade was the American equivalent of twenty-first-century globally televized fund-raising rock concerts. The procession, held in central New York City, attracted as many as one million people. It would be the perfect venue and occasion for Bernays to play his hand.

Following months of careful preparation, Bernays contacted the press. A group of women called "The Torches of Liberty Contingent" were planning an astonishing demonstration in which they would light their "torches of freedom." The journalists were fascinated, and armed with notepads and flashgun cameras they got ready to capture any headline-making news. On a signal, the women produced cigarettes hidden within their layers of clothes and then, with great bravado, publicly lit them. Publicity photos showing the glamorous young insurgents smoking "Torches of Liberty" appeared on the front pages of the world's press.

The taboo was broken and the barriers were down. Women started to buy American Tobacco Company cigarettes. The American Tobacco Company was delighted and rewarded Bernays for his ingenuity by extending his contract. Before long some especially resolute women even went so far as to demand membership in all-male smoking clubs.

Posters reminiscent of Lola Montez's original Boston portrait started appearing everywhere. Within a short time, competitive cigarette manufacturers started to market cigarettes specifically for women. The most notable was Philip Morris, a London-based manufacturer who had opened a New York office in 1902.

Now Philip Morris launched a cigarette brand called Marlboro, specifically aimed at women, and named after the street where its original London factory was situated.

Adverts showing stylish women posed in sophisticated locations featured the slogan, "As mild as May." Copy from a 1924 advert read: "Has smoking any more to do with a woman's morals than the color of her hair?" Much later, in the 1930s, Philip Morris gave the Marlboro brand a refit, changing its filter tip to red so as to be more practical by not smearing lipstick. Later still, the entire brand didn't just go through a relaunch but a sex change (see page 88). As history would eventually reveal, expediency alone would no longer remain the main driving force behind marketing.

3

The hidden truth beneath the dark underbelly of lies

Endure the truth—even if it leaves a bitter taste in your mouth

Ibn Gabirol, Spanish Jewish poet and philosopher (*c.* 1021–1058)

The links between the rich and the rancid are often hidden from public view. This chapter explores how Ivy Ledbetter Lee, one of the founding fathers of political spin, who advised clients to "tell the truth, because sooner or later the public will find out anyway," became the crucial link in hiding the connection between atrocities in World War II, the First Family residing in the White House and some of the world's most powerful oil companies.

As the thunder of World War I gradually receded it was time to face hard truths. Until then it had simply been assumed that consumers would always buy practical and robust products without any need for extensive marketing.

But now, to be desirable, a product had to be more than just practical—it needed to be alluring. Turning products into desires was just the kind of remit that appealed to Edward Bernays. It was also well within the guile and cunning of Ivy Ledbetter Lee, who was by now one of his main advisers.

Back in 1914, Lee's ability to turn adversity into profit had been noticed by the fabulously wealthy Rockefellers. At the time their public image was about as clean as coal after an incident on April 20, 1914. Twenty people, 11 of them children, had died during an attack by the Colorado National Guard against 1,200 striking coal miners and their families. The families were protesting against three of America's biggest mining companies: the Rockefeller-owned Colorado Fuel and Iron Company (CF&I), the Rocky Mountain Fuel Company (RMF), and the Victor-American Fuel Company (VAF). Lee was employed by the Rockefellers "to burnish the family image." Lee advised Rockefeller's son to, "tell the truth, because sooner or later the public will find out anyway. And if the public doesn't like what you are doing, change your policies and bring them into line with what people want."

Years later, Lee was investigated for his work during World War II with the German dye company I. G. Farben. Here lies a web of dubious connections between marketing's soul traders and one of the most evil regimes of the twentieth century. Just one year before Hitler seized power, I. G. Farben donated 400,000 marks to the Nazi Party. During the Nazi regime I. G. Farben held a near-total monopoly on chemical production, including manufacturing Zyklon B, an atrocious poison used as the lethal agent in concentration-camp gas chambers.

In a document dated April 14, 1941 written in Ludwigshafen, Otto Armbrust, the I. G. Farben board member responsible for the Auschwitz project, stated to his board colleagues: "our new friendship with the SS is a blessing. We have determined all measures integrating the concentration camps to benefit our company."

Following World War II the Nuremberg War Crimes Tribunal convicted 24 I. G. Farben board members and executives of mass murder, slavery and other crimes against humanity. The Nuremberg Tribunal dissolved I. G. Farben into Bayer, Hoechst, and BASF. Decades after World War II, BASF, Bayer, and Hoechst (later known as Aventis) each appointed chairmen who were former members of the National Socialist German Workers' Party—or Nationalsozialistische Deutsche Arbeiterpartei (NSDAP), more commonly known as the Nazi Party.

During the war, Carl Wurster, chairman of the board of BASF until 1974, was on the board of the company manufacturing Zyklon B gas. Carl Winnacker, chairman of the board of Hoechst until the late seventies, was a member of the Sturm Abteilung (SA), and on the board of I. G. Farben. Curt Hansen, chairman of the Bayer board until the late seventies, was co-organizer of the conquest of Europe in the department of "acquisition of raw materials."

*A lawyer with his briefcase can steal more than a
hundred men with guns.*

Mario Puzo, *The Godfather*

Lee was not the only member of the Rockefeller entourage to
have dealings with I. G. Farben. John D. Rockefeller himself
also had connections with them. Rockefeller's Standard Oil
Company, later forced by a monopoly ruling to be broken up,
supplied Germany with patents for tetraethyl lead aviation fuel.
Exxon even went into partnership with I. G. Farben. In 1936,
Schroder, Rockefeller's investment bank, included board directors
linked to the Gestapo and European-connected banks. The firm's
lawyers, John Foster Dulles and Allen Dulles, also represented
I. G. Farben.

Between 1953 and 1959, President Dwight D. Eisenhower
appointed John Foster Dulles as American Secretary of State.
His brother Allen eventually became the first civilian (and the
longest-serving) Director of Central Intelligence. Allen was also a
member of the Warren Commission, which published the highly
controversial report on the assassination of President Kennedy.

*America is never wholly herself unless she is engaged
in high moral principle. We as a people have such
a purpose today. It is to make kinder the face of the
nation and gentler the face of the world.*

George H. W. Bush, former President of America

The I. G. Farben controversy reverberated well into the twenty-
first century. In 2004, journalist Duncan Campbell of the *Guardian*
alleged that George Bush's grandfather, the late American senator
Prescott Bush, was a director and shareholder of companies that
profited from working with I. G. Farben. According to American
investigative reporter John Buchanan, this involvement was

allegedly an active, rather than a passive relationship. This claim was supported by files in the American National Archives showing that Prescott Bush was, in his work as a company director, directly involved with the financial supporters of Nazism. Two former Auschwitz slave laborers brought a civil action for $40bn in a compensation claim that the Bush family materially benefited from Auschwitz slave labor during World War II.

According to Buchanan, documents in the Library of Congress relating to the McCormack–Dickstein Committee (1934–5), which collected testimony "on how foreign subversive propaganda entered America along with the organizations that were spreading it," showed that Prescott Bush, the Du Pont family, the Remington family, and J. P. Morgan attempted to assassinate F. D. Roosevelt and put a fascist state in place. According to Buchanan, they were going to round up troublemakers and Jews to put them into internment camps. The coup failed because their chosen military expert, General Smedley D. Butler, betrayed them.

Buchanan asserted that even after the war, many of the group continued to move Nazi assets into Switzerland, Brazil, Argentina and Panama.

In 1951, the American government liquidated the Union Banking Corporation, which managed profits from I. G. Farben. Prescott Bush received $1.5 million for his holdings in the Nazi-associated business. Buchanan stated that this was the beginning of the Bush family fortune. Refuting the claim, in 2003 the Anti-Defamation League in America, who were supportive of Prescott Bush and the Bush family, said that "rumors about the alleged Nazi 'ties' of the late Prescott Bush . . . have circulated widely through the internet in recent years. These charges are untenable and politically motivated . . . Prescott Bush was neither a Nazi nor a Nazi sympathizer." However, one of the country's oldest Jewish publications, the *Jewish Advocate*, aired the controversy in detail.

In 2008, speaking at the Israeli Knesset, President George W. Bush chastized presidential candidate Barack Obama for appeasing terrorists in the same way as people during the build-up to World War II had appeased the Nazi Party. That caused some of the media to "remind" the President of just how much his own family's fortune was gained through financial dealings connected with the infamous I. G. Farben. (At the time of writing, the claim from the former Auschwitz prisoners remains unsettled.)

Back in his heyday, this scenario would have given I. G. Farben's PR adviser Ivy Ledbetter Lee a real run for his money. In addition to his work with Farben, Ledbetter Lee also advised George Westinghouse, one of the pioneers of electricity as well as an early celebrity brand icon; aviator, explorer and peace activist Charles Lindbergh; American politician and lawyer John W. Davis; investment banker and philanthropist Otto Kahn; and the automobile pioneer Walter Chrysler.

4

Talking up the Great Depression

The history of the last century shows, as we shall see later, that the advice given to governments by bankers, like the advice they gave to industrialists, was consistently good for bankers, but was often disastrous for governments, businessmen, and the people generally.

Professor Carroll Quigley, adviser to President Bill Clinton

The American Depression of the 1920s and 1930s left the entire world feeling hopeless, at least until the PR men began to step in with promises of a better deal for all. For the first time during this period, PR was used to help the government manage a recession and also manage companies' images that were otherwise suffering. The early PR men concerned themselves with polishing up the images of politicians and the rich and important men of commerce. They fostered the belief that to rebuild prosperity people had to start spending. They believed a docile market could be made to desire non-essential goods as avidly as essential goods. This sentiment would be virtually repeated 100 years later during another world crisis.

———

While Ivy Ledbetter Lee was polishing up the images of the ostensibly "virtuous and praiseworthy," Bernays was more concerned in shaping the image of the commercially powerful and wealthy. He helped William Randolph Hearst, the newspaper magnate later mythologized in the movie *Citizen Kane*, sell women's magazines. By getting movie stars like Clara Bow to be photographed in the magazines using products made by his other clients, Bernays showed how the "Visual Association Value" (VAV) could help to associate products with desirable celebrities. And so the world was introduced to the celebrity brand icon.

Hearst probably understood the marketing and newspaper business better than anyone. He certainly knew how to "hook" readers and so secure sales. He once said: "News is what someone somewhere doesn't want you to read. The rest is advertising." It would become a famous aphorism quoted regularly by modern-day spin doctors.

Bernays convinced psychologists to publish independent reports stating that his clients' products were good for people. Back in the days of the Creel Committee, Bernays called such manipulation, "The Engineering of Consent." In 1947 he wrote: "If we understand the mechanism and motives of the group mind, is it not possible to control and regiment the masses according to our will without their knowing about it?"

Believing that you could control the irrational selfishness of people by satisfying them with highly desirable consumer products, Bernays used VAVs to help bolster the image of the relatively mild-mannered President Coolidge (1923–29), creating the world's first media-savvy president. Bernays ensured the 30th president was always available to reporters. He even had his own political slogan, "Keep cool with Coolidge."

A photograph of President Coolidge sent from New York to London on November 29, 1924 became the first photo picture reproduced by transoceanic radio facsimile, or fax. Coolidge delivered 529 press conferences—more than any president before. His inauguration was the first to be broadcast on radio. Coolidge was even filmed on the White House lawn by Lee DeForest, so becoming the first president to appear in a sound movie, *President Coolidge, Taken on the White House Lawn.*

If I had asked people what they wanted, they would have said faster horses

Henry T. Ford, founder of the Ford Motor Company

A contented consumer coveting desirable but not essential wants rather than practical needs, made for a docile mass market that could be easily manipulated by the very same organizations feeding their wishes. To rebuild prosperity after the war years, people had to start spending. The era of mass factory production had to be lubricated with consumer needs for more and more goods.

Entrepreneurs with a natural knack for marketing, such as Walter L. Jacobs, recognized opportunities for mass-produced goods like cars. In 1918, starting with only 12 Model T Fords, Jacobs opened a car-rental operation in Chicago. The business soon expanded to the point where, within five years, it generated annual revenues of about $1 million. In 1923, Jacobs sold his car-rental concern to John Hertz, President of Yellow Cab and Yellow Truck and Coach Manufacturing Company. Jacobs continued as Hertz's top operating and administrative executive. The rental business called Hertz Drive-Ur-Self System was acquired in 1926 by General Motors Corporation, when it bought Yellow Truck from John Hertz. Today Hertz operates from approximately 7,700 locations in 145 countries worldwide.

But as with any major recession, while a few prospered, the majority were happy to simply survive. In 1928, Republican presidential candidate Herbert Hoover ran a campaign promise of a "chicken in every pot and two cars in every garage." Filling that garage and pot meant running up huge debts. Demand dwindled. Profits failed to be passed on to consumers. Products like the Ford Model T were ubiquitous; in fact there was a glut of everything.

With barely enough cash to purchase everyday essentials, layoffs began. Unemployment rose. Unregulated banks, which had gambled depositors' money on the stock exchange, experienced a reversal of fortune. Loans to enable investors to buy shares couldn't be repaid. In an attempt to drive the American economy forward, high import duties on European goods meant that foreign trade with America was no longer commercially viable. To finance the shortfall, Europe was coerced into borrowing more money from America. However, with little consumer spending going on within America there was hardly any money left in the proverbial pot. The result: a total economic system crash.

Thirty-two thousand American businesses folded in 1932 alone. From late 1929 to mid-1932, 5,000 banks folded, losing $3.2 billion of deposits. By 1933, 13 million American people were unemployed. Poor workers had had enough. Necessary economic-led layoffs meant that huge corporations like the American steel industry went full-out to prevent organized trade unions creating tremendous headaches.

It was a public relations man, John Wiley Hill, who offered the American steel industry a PR campaign to manage their public image. In the 1937 Republic Steel Massacre, steel company security officers opened fire on pro-union demonstrators, slaughtering ten people. Hill ensured that thousands of leaflets claiming that the "cops" were forced to fire in self-defence and that the unions were communist sympathizers were distributed.

While men like Hill used PR to clean up images, the economy as a whole was still in a mess. It cost farmers more to harvest and transport their products than they could earn from actually selling them. In response, the government set up the Farm Board to buy up surplus farm produce. It made little difference. The American countryside reeked with the stench of rotting cattle flesh and incinerated carcasses. Thousands were left homeless. A stubborn president refused to offer financial relief. Poverty led to undernourishment. Even the birth rate tumbled as marriages were postponed.

Mob rule was in the ascent. It was the era of the Angry Mob and time for a new deal and a new president. A new president would need to start from scratch, and implement a system to accurately measure whether the economy was shrinking or growing. This was a task eventually delegated to the economist Simon Kuznets, who devised a standardized accounting system to measure national performance—the GNP, or Gross National Product.

With an accurate way of monitoring the economy, the newly-elected President Roosevelt took up the ideas of one of the original

Creel Committee members, Walter Lippmann. Lippmann saw the public in the same light as the philosopher Plato, as "a great beast or a bewildered herd—floundering in the chaos of local opinions." Lippmann believed citizens should be governed by an elite class consisting of experts, specialists and bureaucrats, whose interests reach beyond the locality, and who had lost the moral high ground by succumbing to desires rather than needs.

Roosevelt promised relief from poverty and the recovery of industry, including close monitoring of the stock market and removal of the Gold Standard. He also set out to reform employment and welfare.

> "Rulers of the exchange of mankind's goods have failed through their own stubbornness and incompetence, they have admitted their failure, and have abdicated. Practices of the unscrupulous moneychangers stand indicted in the court of public opinion, rejected by the hearts and minds of men. True they have tried, but their efforts have been cast in the pattern of an outworn tradition. Faced by failure of credit they have proposed only the lending of more money. Stripped of the lure of profit by which to induce our people to follow their false leadership, they have resorted to exhortations, pleading tearfully for restored confidence . . . The moneychangers have fled from their high seats in the temple of our civilization. We may now restore that temple to the ancient truths. The measure of the restoration lies in the extent to which we apply social values more noble than mere monetary profit."
> (Franklin D. Roosevelt, March 4, 1933)

Yet, like the confused electorate chasing promised dreams, while much was achieved during the Roosevelt administration's first 100 days the New Deal was, for the most part, a disappointment. This wasn't down to any lack of zeal on Roosevelt's part. He established Alphabet Agencies (named after their A–Z acronyms) that provided employment support. He suspended all war debts for one year. Yet still the New Deal had more hope than substance. Long-term unemployment wasn't curtailed. Thirty percent of the black American underclass remained on the poverty line. Apart from cheap manual labour, women, who only a few years earlier had ignited their "Torches of Liberty," remained largely unemployed. Yet despite all this, the President's resolute determination to turn things around was gaining approval in some very unlikely places.

5

The evil men do . . .

By the skillful and sustained use of propaganda, one can make a people see even heaven as hell or an extremely wretched life as paradise.

Adolf Hitler

In the 1930s and 1940s, during propaganda's bleakest and most corrupt period, the German authorities turned ordinary people's desires for unity into a force for depravity. Heading the strategy was one of the world's most morally corrupt, yet socially perceptive masterminds—Joseph Goebbels. His legacy was the awful truth that, using the right kind of media and given the right circumstances, conditions and opportunity, any person, however "civilized" or well educated, can be led to do and believe anything—however evil it may appear in hindsight.

Disturbingly, many of the products and marketing techniques specifically designed to exemplify the Nazi utopian dream still survive—although they are now used in the service of a different kind of world order.

Like America, Germany had both feet stuck in the muddy quagmire of the Depression. Germany's industrial production was roughly equal to that in America. However, two young men living in Germany took a very different view on the state of the world economy. One was born into a strict Catholic family and was a graduate in history and literature from the University of Heidelberg. The other was a wide-eyed youth besotted with a pretty girl whose surname suggests Jewish roots. Later he secured work as a jobbing artist brushing out bland but respectable picture-postcard artworks. It dawned on him that his artistic career was going nowhere.

The artist was Adolf Hitler. The graduate was Joseph Goebbels. Surprisingly, Goebbels not only recognized but openly admired President Roosevelt. Goebbels said:

"I am very interested in social developments in America. I believe Roosevelt has chosen the right path. We are dealing with the greatest social problem ever known. Millions of unemployed must get their jobs back and this cannot be left to private initiative. It is the government that must solve the problem."

But Goebbels' admiration was misplaced and warped. Whilst Roosevelt believed that government should consider the people's feelings, Goebbels supposed that democracy was in fact a dangerously irresponsible force that, given free rein, simply unleashed self-interested individualism. Goebbels shared Bernays' and Lippmann's view that such independence was ultimately a destructive energy in dire need of careful and incisive stage-management.

It is the cause, not the death that makes the martyr

Napoleon Bonaparte

To manage such a reckless force, Goebbels had to give the German people some kind of distraction. His first diversion came in the shape of a person presented to take on the sins of society's wrongdoers and in doing so be turned into a national brand icon. That person was Horst Ludwig Wessel.

Wessel was an enthusiastic member of the German National People's Party (DNVP) and the Bismarckjugend youth group, before joining the Nazi Party in 1926. In 1929, Wessel wrote lyrics for a Nazi battle song. Goebbels approved of the song, "Die Fahne Hoch," and published it. One cold January night in 1930, on answering his front door Wessel was shot squarely in the face. His alleged assailant was Albrecht (Aly) Höhler, a keen activist for the local Communist Party (KPD) branch. Höhler was sentenced to six years. In 1933 the Gestapo murdered him.

Turning Wessel's death into a propaganda opportunity, Goebbels arranged for a funeral to be attended by 30,000 people.

Reports in *Die Brünnen*, the official party journal, said: "How high Horst Wessel towers over that Jesus of Nazareth—that Jesus who pleaded that the bitter cup be taken from him. How unattainably high all Horst Wessels stand above Jesus!" Goebbels also commissioned books and movies idealising Wessel's short life. Town squares were named after him. In 1936, a three-mast training ship—the *Horst Wessel*—was commissioned. Curiously, it was later captured by the American Navy, renamed the USCGC *Eagle*, and is still in service as a training cutter for the American Coast Guard.

Although officially banned in Germany, even today many underground right-wing political parties continue to sing the Horst Wessel song:

". . . The street free for the brown battalions; the street free for the Storm-Trooper. Up at the swastika millions already look, full of hope; The day breaks for freedom and for bread. For the last time the call will now be blown. For the struggle we all stand ready. Soon will fly Hitler-flags over every street. Slavery will last only a short time longer."
"The Horst Wessel Song," 1929

We're all going on a Sommerferien

As well as rehabilitating thugs as martyrs, Goebbels became involved with, of all things, marketing the German tourism business. Set up in November 1933, KdF (*Kraft durch Freude*— Strength through Joy), the Third Reich's official state-controlled leisure organization, promoted the advantages of National Socialism to the German people. In the 1930s it grew into the world's largest tourism operator.

KdF offered a comprehensive program of benefits and amenities to the German working class and their families. These included subsidized holidays at resorts across Germany as well as in "safe" countries abroad. Particularly Italy, whose "jolly," rotund host was a certain Benito Amilcare Andrea Mussolini. KdF even marketed the world's first purpose-built cruise liners: the *Wilhelm Gustloff* and the *Robert Ley*—built to carry KdF members in style on luxurious Mediterranean holidays.

Other KdF-led programs included concerts, opera, free physical education, and gymnastics. In fact, by all accounts, KdF was one of the Nazi regime's most popular programs. By marketing its image as a benevolent organization, KdF played an essential role in reconciling the working class to the Nazi regime.

Think small

Volkswagen slogan

KdF collaborated with the manufacturers DAF to teach capitalist America a lesson or two in mass production of cars for the common man. Hitler, who admired cars but couldn't drive, asked DAF to subsidise and provide a "*Volks*" (People's) car that that could sell for less than 1,000 Reichsmarks. A marketing program was launched with the slogan: "*Fünf Mark die Woche musst Du sparen, willst Du im eigenen Wagen fahren*" ("Save five Marks a week, if you want to drive your own car"). The vehicle was designed by Ferdinand Porsche to be safe, economical, and easy to drive.

A Volkswagen VW Käfer (known to us now as the VW Beetle) was promised to any German worker who could scrimp and save for special stamps. The first models rolled off the production line in February 1939. Yet despite all the efforts of the industrious workers, not one of them ever received a vehicle. However, a Type 1 Cabriolet was presented as a 49th-birthday present to Hitler on April 20, 1938.

Thanks to smart marketing, decades later the Volkswagen Beetle went on to be rebranded as an icon representing peace and generally "groovy" chic happiness.

It is by manipulating "hidden forces" that the advertising experts induce us to buy their wares—a toothpaste, a brand of cigarettes, a political candidate. And it is by appealing to the same hidden forces—and others too dangerous for Madison Avenue to meddle with—that Hitler induced the German masses to buy themselves a Fuehrer, an insane philosophy and the Second World War.

Aldous Huxley, *Brave New World Revisited*

As head of a specially created National Ministry for Public Enlightenment and Propaganda, Goebbels became president of a newly formed Chamber of Culture for the Reich. The Chamber had seven subchambers, overseeing fine arts, music, theatre, the press, radio, and literature. In 1933 there were 4,700 daily German newspapers, 3 percent controlled by the Nazi Party. By 1944 there were 997 daily newspapers in circulation, of which the Nazis controlled 82 percent. The Ministry for Enlightenment and Propaganda instructed editors on placing articles. In fact the Nazi Press Agency supplied an estimated 50 percent of all editorial content, overseen by Goebbels.

(Although not directly connected with our story of the Nazi Press Agency, it is interesting to note that the word "editor" was originally introduced by another regime—the Roman Empire. Roman editors working in propaganda theatres like the Colosseum arranged propaganda spectacles, such as gladiator fights, or incredible staged presentations of wild animals and trophies captured by the sprawling Roman Empire. In one such show for the citizens of Rome, a full-size replica of a whale was levered up to the arena floor. Thousands of wild animals were marched out from its mouth.)

Key media controlled by the Ministry for Enlightenment and Propaganda

Radio: Wardens were appointed to report on people's reactions to specific broadcasts. Cheap radios (*Volksempfänger*, or people's receivers) were distributed. These were adapted to prevent foreign broadcasts. Between 1932 and 1939 the number of families with radios rose from 25 percent to 70 percent.

Movies: The Nazi government bought up shares in four major national movie companies. By 1942 all movie companies were totally state-controlled. Over 1,000 propaganda movies were produced during the Third Reich.

Music: Jewish composers including Mahler and Mendelssohn were banned. Modernist composers such as Stravinsky and Schoenberg had scorn poured upon them. Jazz was labeled Negroid and degenerate.

Where books are burned, human beings are destined to be burned too.

Heinrich Heine

Literature: On May 10, 1933 in Berlin's central square, the largest book-burning event in history took place. Public and private libraries were raided. All available Jewish, socialist or pacifist books were destroyed. Speaking at the rally, Goebbels said:

". . . The era of extreme Jewish intellectualism is now at an end. The breakthrough of the German revolution has again cleared the way on the German path . . . The future German man will not just be a man of books, but a man of character. It is to this end that we want to educate you. As a young person, to already have the courage to face the pitiless glare, to overcome the fear of death, and to regain respect for death—this is the task of this young generation.

And thus you do well in this midnight hour to commit to the flames the evil spirit of the past. This is a strong, great and symbolic deed—a deed which should document the following for the world to know. Here the intellectual foundation of the November [democratic] Republic is sinking to the ground, but from this wreckage the phoenix of a new spirit will triumphantly rise."

The speech and book burning were accompanied by the singing of Nazi songs, including Wessel's "Die Fahne Hoch" and other anthems.

Art: In 1933, Goebbels issued a five-point manifesto describing "What German artists can expect from the new government." It listed the following guidance:

- All works of a cosmopolitan or Bolshevist nature should be removed from German museums and collections, but first they should be exhibited to the public, who should be informed of the details of their acquisition, and then burned.
- All museum directors who "wasted" public monies by purchasing "un-German" art should be fired immediately.
- No artist with Marxist or Bolshevist connections should be mentioned henceforth.
- No box-like buildings should be built.
- All public sculptures not "approved" by the German public should be immediately removed.

Art critics were answerable to the state and from 1936 could only provide "descriptive reviews." Certain styles of art were given political labels, for example Alfred Rosenberg (one of the main authors of Nazi ideology) described expressionism as "Bolshevik filth." In 1937 two parallel art exhibitions were held in Munich, one representing what the Nazi regime viewed as the best of German art (Grosse Deutsche Kunstausstellung); the other displayed what was deemed as "degenerate art" (Entartete Kunst). In 1937 Goebbels confiscated over 16,000 works that were considered "degenerate." Many of the works were sold to foreign art buyers to make money for the Reich.

In 1937 the degenerate art exhibition was opened in Munich. Two million people attended the show. The event featured haphazardly displayed art considered to be un-German or "Jewish Bolshevist." The term "Jewish Bolshevist" was spread globally in the 1920s with the circulation of *The Protocols of the Elders of Zion*, a partly plagiarized, completely fabricated and subsequently totally disregarded book that alleged an unfounded Jewish plot to take over the world. The Nazis drew partly on the spurious book as a validation for wiping out all Jewish businesses and property, leading to the slaughter of six million people.

In 1988 another group with little regard for their own civilians and who were also masters of propaganda spin and disinformation adopted the Protocols: the Sunni Islamist paramilitary movement Hamas. One quote from Hamas' charter read: "The time will not come until Muslims will fight the Jews; until the Jews hide behind rocks and trees, which will cry: O Muslim! There is a Jew hiding behind me, come on and kill him . . ."

Rallies

Hitler would be chauffeured in an open-top car down winding streets and large highways named after him. Suitably impressive buildings dedicated to the new Nazi culture featured in this new urban architecture. Rallies were choreographed under the creative direction of Albert Speer, whose imposing structures were featured in Goebbels' propaganda movies such as *Triumph des Willens* (Triumph of the Will). Rallies featured dramatic lighting effects, smart tailored uniforms, and banners. The highly manipulated political-spin presentational techniques helped shape German perceptions of what it was to be Germanic, offering aspirations of a brave new nation united under one banner of red, white, and black, instilling a sense of hope and prosperity.

For good measure, the President of the Chamber of Culture manufactured incontrovertible laws of history that drew on his academic past to make unfounded historical parallels with Nazi philosophy. Goebbels kept things simple and on message. Explaining his strategy he said:

> "If you tell a lie big enough and keep repeating it, people will eventually come to believe it. The lie can be maintained only for such time as the State can shield the people from the political, economic and/or military consequences of the lie. It thus becomes vitally important for the State to use all of its powers to repress dissent, for the truth is the mortal enemy of the lie, and thus by extension, the truth is the greatest enemy of the State . . . The most brilliant propagandist technique will yield no success unless one fundamental principle is borne in mind constantly—it must confine itself to a few points and repeat them over and over."

The irony of this statement is that Goebbels turned the notion of the lie—a concept described by Hitler in his book *Mein Kampf*—on its head from being something used by an enemy of the State into something that could be used by the State.

Hitler originally wrote:

> ". . . In this they [Jews] proceeded on the sound principle that the magnitude of a lie always contains a certain factor of credibility, since the great masses of the people in the very bottom of their hearts tend to be corrupted rather than consciously and purposely evil, and that, therefore,

in view of the primitive simplicity of their minds they more easily fall a victim to a big lie than to a little one, since they themselves lie in little things, but would be ashamed of lies that were too big. Such a falsehood will never enter their heads and they will not be able to believe in the possibility of such monstrous effrontery and infamous misrepresentation in others; yes, even when enlightened on the subject, they will long doubt and waver, and continue to accept at least one of these causes as true. Therefore, something of even the most insolent lie will always remain and stick—a fact which all the great lie-virtuosi and lying-clubs in this world know only too well and also make the most treacherous use of. The foremost connoisseurs of this truth regarding the possibilities in the use of falsehood and slander have always been the Jews; for after all, their whole existence is based on one single great lie, to wit, that they are a religious community while actually they are a race— and what a race!"

Adolf Hitler, *Mein Kampf*

In 1941, Goebbels turned the notion of "the big lie" around. Referring to Winston Churchill, he wrote in *Die Zeit ohne Beispiel*: "The English follow the principle that when one lies, one should lie big, and stick to it. They keep up their lies, even at the risk of looking ridiculous."

The dual approach of passive initiatives such as KdF linked with attempts to manipulate the people with repetitive political messages made Nazi ideals memorable and rewarding. However, such methods could only ever temporarily spur the German people into action. Goebbels needed something more pervasive. He turned again to the concepts of Bernays, who would later describe his disgust at the thought of Goebbels' wicked corruption of his ideas.

What luck for rulers that men do not think

Adolf Hitler

In America, Bernays spoke Freud's view that, given the right emotional cues from an impassioned leader as well as a specific target for their irrational belligerence, crowds could be whipped into a frenzy of irrationality if allowed to freely express themselves.

Goebbels believed that the human being is basically a destructive animal. Time after time, history taught that in order to realize a higher philosophical goal, mankind found expression through the natural release of primeval instincts. To promote his case against the Jews as an "outsider" enemy, Goebbels spotted a publicity stunt in America carried out by the author Theodore N. Kaufman, who had published a book called *Germany Must Perish!*. The stunt involved sending a miniature black cardboard coffin to reviewers. Inside the casket a card read: "Read GERMANY MUST PERISH! Tomorrow you will receive your copy." The 104-page book alleged that Jews were plotting against Germany. Goebbels' imagination was kindled. Not only would this stunt help prove that the Jews were the German people's mortal enemy, but it would help consolidate the idea that the whole of America was to be distrusted.

Meanwhile in America, whilst many were watching the developments in Germany with increasing alarm, some White House officials were becoming more and more interested in the idea that propaganda could have uses much closer to home.

6

Living the brand ideal

Happy days are here again

Franklin D. Roosevelt political slogan, 1932

Walk into any modern shopping mall or center and you step into a world of brand ideals offering tantalizing promises of consumer bliss for the price of a new outfit, washing machine or even a Starbucks coffee. Many manufacturers like Apple have turned retail stores into brand experiences where like-minded people searching for a sense of identity can meet, discuss and above all, spend . . . spend . . . Spend! The establishment of modern commercially run fantasy dream-parks like Disney World and even brand-sponsored Olympic Games owes much to a plan devised in 1939 to build a world stage for America Inc.

While Nazi Party fanatics in Germany were trying to erase history by burning books and preparing to annihilate innocent men, women and children, President Roosevelt decided to meet with the founder of the American Institute of Public Opinion— George Gallup.

Using sophisticated survey methods and a sample of only 5,000, Gallup had correctly predicted the results of the presidential election, in contrast to the *Literary Digest* magazine, which asked two million people their election intentions and yet still managed to get the results wrong by a mile. Gallup told Roosevelt that contrary to Bernays' opinion of the people being little more than an unruly mob, the American people were in fact level-headed citizens.

This consoled the President, who was concerned about his failing grip on power. Since advertised products and services were becoming more appealing to the American people, advertising was seen as offering a way of reaching a public that was disenchanted with politics . . .

Roosevelt would have to redouble his soul-trading efforts. Part of his strategy was to commission propaganda movies carefully scripted to demonize the commercial world as misguided corporate PR men and selfish business clients who, while purporting to care for the individual man and woman, were actually far more concerned with the profit columns in their sales books.

Such dirty political tactics required the commercial community to pitch back an equally hard-hitting response. The task was handed to a cluster of American corporations called the National Association of Manufacturers (NAM). The group maintained that while Roosevelt may have believed in the power of sagacity, given the right interpretation, the ideas of Bernays offered a far greater and much more persuasive force. The NAM felt (as would generations of soul traders who followed them) that the majority of people assumed that while individual discrete emotions such as sadness, happiness, and anger couldn't be controlled, actions to temper such emotional effects could. With a little creative emotional management, these seemingly unmanageable actions could be far more easily manipulated than most people imagined.

The NAM devised an extraordinary scheme, based on Bernays' strategies to create an emotional attachment between the public and corporate America. This idea of "emotional attachment" turned feature-led Unique Selling Propositions (USPs) into what marketers would decades later know as intuitively driven Emotional Selling Propositions (ESPs). Millions of dollars were invested in a campaign designed to prove that rather than owing their gratitude to the White House, the American people owed everything, including the essence of what it really was to be an American, to the real champions who built "the land of the free." It was industrious businesses along with honest, tough, wonderful consumers who were turning the American dream into a reality, not the politicians.

We are in the same tents as the clowns and the freaks—that's show business

Edward R. Murrow, American broadcast journalist

Bernays devised a plan directly linking the pursuit of democracy with the newly repositioned goals of America Inc. These goals and aspirations would form the cornerstones of "the world of tomorrow," embodied in the World's Fair of 1939 held in New York, the world's most awe-inspiring capital.

The organization tasked with implementing this plan was called the New York World's Fair Corporation. Grover Whalen, a PR specialist, presided over a committee consisting of carefully chosen notables such as Winthrop Aldrich, the President of Chase National Bank, Mortimer Buckner, who had been President of the New York Trust Company, John J. Dunnigan, the politician and architect, Harvey Dow Gibson, former President of the Liberty Bank of New York, Fiorello La Guardia, the Mayor of New York, and Percy S. Straus from the department store Macys.

Part-trade show, part-League of Nations, part-amusement park, and even part-utopian community, the World's Fair promoted its message of hope and prosperity through a combination of provocative imagery and imaginative practical presentations featuring consumer icons, symbols, exhibitions, and product demonstrations. From top to bottom, everything about the World's Fair was designed to impress and intrigue. A 210m (700ft) sphere dominated the fair. Special movie theatres were erected showing propaganda movies presenting "happy farmers and workers."

A sprawling landscape of so-called "democracities" was built. Derelict ground was resurfaced with perfectly paved streets, with such names as the "Avenue of Patriots," "Constitution Mall," the "Avenue of Pioneers," and "Avenue of Labor." Locations housed imposing buildings including the Court of Communications. Buildings were crowned with the Stars and Stripes, beneath which inspired people could walk a path of hope acknowledging the support of business and a vision of technological enterprise.

General Motors promised cars that would enable motorists to reach and navigate around a promised brave new world. This crude but poignant message helped change the face and the scale of advertising and marketing. It reshaped American perceptions of what it was to be American and told individuals how they could contribute towards building a nation in which anyone could be proud to own such an icon of American values.

At the time, Walter Lippmann wrote: "General Motors has spent a small fortune to convince the American public that if it wishes to enjoy the full benefits of private enterprise in motor manufacturing, it will have to rebuild its cities and its highways by public enterprise."

The Ford exposition featured a winding, half-mile road named the "Road of Tomorrow." Ford propaganda movies highlighted the differences between car production by hand and machine production; the movie's narrator said: "Machinery creates cars at prices that people can pay, and creates millions of jobs in the process."

The American Telephone & Telegraph (AT&T) exhibition demonstrated advancements in person-to-person and long-distance calling. A prominent sign read, "Demonstration telephone calls to any one of the 16,000,000 telephones of the Bell System and to any of the 4,200,000 telephones of the other companies in the United States," before continuing to stress that AT&T was four times bigger and better than its competitors.

Radio provided Americans an ear to the world at home and abroad. It offered families the chance to listen to President Roosevelt's fireside chats. RCA's (Radio Corporation of America) new communication device to the world was TV. Public TV broadcasting flickered into life in the New York City area on the same day as the Fair: a "coincidental" publicity coup.

Three mechanically scanned TV cameras photographed the world's first TV broadcast, "The Queen's Messenger." Two actors spoke their lines on camera, while two others acted as hand models for close-ups. The broadcast was seen on a total of four 41-line TV sets in Schenectady, New York, the home of General Electric.

United States Steel Corporation, Glass Incorporated and the Consolidated Edison Company demonstrated a "better living through science" exhibit. Westinghouse, producers of refrigerators and dishwashers, aggressively marketed their products to women with contests offering an easier and more leisurely way of life with machines.

A movie shown at the fair, *The Middleton Family at the New York World's Fair*, told of a perfect average American family's visit to the fair. An ideal family unit, the Middletons were role models who explained what, where and when to buy 100 percent American goods. The Middletons marvelled at the dishwashing contest in the Westinghouse building in which Mrs. Modern, a Westinghouse character, washed her pots and pans with a Westinghouse dishwasher, whilst a ridiculed Mrs. Drudge slowly performed chores by hand, losing the contest and ending up less "neat and refreshed than when she started."

Other structures of note at the World's Fair included the Heinz Dome, the Beech-Nut Packing building and the Schaefer Center, in which a restaurant accommodated 1,600 hungry consumers eager to bite into American mustard-topped wieners. The American Tobacco Company Building took the shape of a giant pack of Lucky Strike cigarettes.

By the time the fair opened, Britain and France had declared war on Germany. With such a delicate balance of world affairs, at the last moment the Soviet pavilion, the second-largest structure in the fair featuring gigantic portraits of Lenin and Stalin, was replaced with a lawn called the "American Common."

It's quite fun to do the impossible
Walt Disney

On July 17, 1955, over a decade later, the world's greatest-ever monument to brand ideals in the guise of a fantasy world opened. Instead of streets like "The Road of Tomorrow" and "Avenue of the Patriots," this new brand wonderland featured areas such as "Tomorrow Land" and "Main Street USA." The brand utopia was Disney World™ in Florida. By 2008 the theme park had attracted in excess of 515 million visitors. Disney went on to build Disneyland in Los Angeles, Tokyo Disney Resort, and Disneyland Resort Paris, as well as many other brand ventures including a cruise-line company.

The World's Fair was amongst the first major semi-state-sponsored brand experiences of its kind. Decades after visitors at the World's Fair took up banners in one hand and munched a hotdog with the other, or families first shook hands with Mickey Mouse in Disney World, or the British public celebrated their war victory at the Festival of Britain in 1951, a new propaganda folly was built. This time it had the blessing of both the government and big business.

A national political campaign is better than the best circus ever heard of, with a mass baptism and a couple of hangings thrown in.
Henry Louis Mencken, American journalist

The Millennium Dome was a folly built on the derelict wasteland at London's Docklands to celebrate the start of the new millennium. It opened to the public on the eve of the twenty-first century. The semi-permanent structure cost its state-sponsored owners, the New Millennium Experience Company, £789 million, of which £628 million was covered by National Lottery grants and £189 million was raised through ticket sales. As with the World's Fair of 1939, special zones were designed as tributes to benevolent brands that encouraged suitably awe-inspired consumers to anticipate a better and brighter future.

At the time, the British Prime Minister, Tony Blair, enthusiastically said: "In the Dome we have a creation that, I believe, will truly be a beacon to the world."[1] But in the end, by popular consensus the Dome represented little more than a PR fiasco rather than a propaganda triumph. Under state management it raised neither emotional confidence nor sufficient funds to cover its heating costs. It was eventually sold to the private entertainment company Anschutz Entertainment Group, which went on to sell the name rights for the venue to the telecoms company O2. At the time of writing, the center is used as a brand ambassador for O2, hosting world-class entertainment acts.

Bow down before entering your brand place of worship

The Dome inspired other trader "cathedrals" to venerate brand names encouraging consumers to experience a sense of belonging and meaning. As well as educating the public about a company's history or products, such venues gave ample opportunities to buy household-name products in conveniently located gift stores often featuring displays designed to remind visitors of a brand's values. The venues included:

Guinness Storehouse® in Dublin, Ireland
Nike Towns (more retail stores than brand educational establishments, strategically located throughout the world)
Hershey's Chocolate World in Philadelphia, America
Volkswagen's Autostadt in Wolfsburg, Germany
World of Coca-Cola in Atlanta, America
Ethel M. Chocolate Factory in Las Vegas, America

Cadbury World in Bournville, England.
NBC Studio Tour in New York, America
Anheuser-Busch Brewery in St Louis, America
Corning Museum of Glass in New York, America
Heineken Experience in Amsterdam, the Netherlands
Crayola Factory in Philadelphia, America

Hovering around position number three (at the time of writing) of the world's most popular brand venues was the Guinness Storehouse®. It was marketed as a friendly day out offering fun and vibrancy. Explaining the brand thinking behind the venue, Guinness's marketing department explained that the underlining purpose of the venue was to "immerse our audience in a compelling Guinness experience." The commercial objective was to "convert everyone we touch into Guinness Ambassadors . . . leaving with a sense of belonging, having received the warmest of welcomes in the 'Home of Guinness®'—the national drink." Pitched as the only "Home of Guinness®," the Guinness Storehouse® was meant to leave visitors with an experience beyond replication. "Its contemporary feel is reflected both in the building and use of technology," says a slide from a promotional PowerPoint presentation.

According to research conducted in March 2008 by Red C Research, 89 percent of all visitors who went to the Guinness Storehouse® tried a pint at the venue. Of these visitors, 85 percent were irregular Guinness® drinkers and 26 percent were first-time Guinness® drinkers. Yet 72 percent of visitors leaving the Guinness Storehouse® said they felt "closer to the brand."

But as a conscientious company, Diageo, owner of the Guinness® brand, was in an awkward position when it came to encouraging responsible drinking. A member of leading NGOs and SAOs including the International Centre for Alcohol Policies (ICAP), the European Forum for Responsible Drinking, the

Portman Group, DISCUS and the Century Council, it was keen to promote responsible drinking. A 2008 report from the British Department of Health, although not naming Diageo, did allege widespread abuse of the voluntary drinks industry code on alcohol. The official government report said that ten million Britons regularly drank in excess of government guidelines. Alcohol abuse was costing the British government £25 billion a year in policing, social services and lost working hours. Annual hospital admissions from alcohol-related conditions such as liver disease, alcohol poisoning, and mental and behavioral disorders shot to a staggering 811,000. The rise in admissions reflected an increase in alcohol consumption per head of 60 percent between 1970 and 2006. According to Alcohol Concern, econometric studies in America found that local drinks advertising was associated with higher levels of drinking among young people in an area.

Apple to the core

While not a one-off experience, another brand cathedral attracting devotees was the Apple Store. Apple concierges in bright T-shirts greet loyal brand devotees like priests welcoming congregants at the imposing "cathedral" gates. As if discussing their messianic leader, dedicated Apple congregants (consumers) cite the company president's views on technology or confess computing sins to Apple trained consultants. Some discuss rumors of the "second coming" of a new model.

Standing out on high streets, Apple Stores are bold, individual, confident, sophisticated, stylish and intrepid. In one weekend alone during 2008, Apple sold one million newly released iPhones. The stores echo much of Apple's ethos, which is clearly reflected in some of its past advertising slogans:

"Soon there will be two kinds of people: Those who use computers, and those who use Apples." (early 1980s)

"The computer for the rest of us." (1984)

"It just works." (2006)

"iThink, therefore iMac." (1998)

One slogan repositioned the company from being spurned as outsiders from the general computer community to being accepted for their independence. "Think different" was devised in 1997 by Los Angles advertising agency TBWA/Chiat/Day. The slogan was thought to have been cocking a snoot at IBM—at the time the number one in IT. IBM's president, Thomas J. Watson, had coined the motto "Think" whilst managing the sales and advertising department at National Cash Register—later to become IBM.

Realizing that in order for the slogan to be effective, it had to deliver more than words, Apple's marketers put their claims into practice, proving "difference" in terms of design, software and service.

For consumers, brand-experience concept stores featuring the lifestyle values lying behind everything from watches to bath soaps slowly appeared everywhere. Each put customer service and fashion style before the more "tacky" business of sales. The walk-through brand sets were designed for consumers seeking a sense of purpose in a world based on materialism. Thanks to brand cathedrals, soul traders were able to offer such consumers a means of temporary escape to an idyll where they could discover a sense of self through the adored brand.

Brand cathedrals painted a perfect win-win scenario for everyone. Consumers got a sense of worth and soul traders got to stage never-ending processions of new and improved brand offers.

Whether it was the World's Fair of 1939, the Virgin London Marathon, or the sponsored British Olympic Games, all brand-experience events were designed to develop a relationship with the consumer, establishing the brand as the preferred choice over and above any competitor.

7

Marketing?
It's all in the mind

We are taught to lose our curiosity by the bludgeon-blows of mass marketing, which brainwash us to see "hits" and discourage exploration

Roger Ebert, American movie screenwriter

Ideas from psychology have always influenced marketing and propaganda. Understanding human psychology is crucial for successfully influencing people's choices and decisions. Companies try to achieve brand loyalty and some have "brand cathedrals" and concept stores to build their image and develop a relationship with customers. But experience shows that people are unpredictable; customers can be fickle, suddenly changing their loyalty to a brand, and a customer's reasons for making a choice are multilayered and complex. In today's world, politicians and businesses may try to influence opinion, but how people react to threats like the credit crunch and global warming, and how they respond to brand icons and national figureheads, can be totally unexpected.

Any commercial spectacular, including the 1939 World's Fair, is a marketing opportunity to win customers looking to choose a favored brand proposition. Bernays, like the marketers who would follow him, believed that choice was influenced by a battle to win over the heart and, more importantly the mind, of the consumer.

Freud wrote, "The ego is not master in its own house." The ego was one-third of a trio of influences: the ego, super-ego, and id. Explaining the id, Freud said:

"It is the dark, inaccessible part of our personality, what little we know of it we have learnt from our study of the dream-work and of the construction of neurotic symptoms, and most of this is of a negative character and can be described only as a contrast to the ego. We approach the id with analogies: we call it a chaos, a cauldron full of seething excitations . . . It is filled with energy reaching it from the instincts, but it has no organization . . . only a striving to bring about the satisfaction of the instinctual needs subject to the observance of the pleasure principle."

Freud classified the id into life (eros—the libidinal energy of love) and death instincts (thanatos). Life instincts addressed pleasurable survival such as sex, food, and status. Death instincts dealt with unconscious wishes to die or put a stop to everyday struggles. The desire for peace was one interpretation of thanatos. Hollywood escapism and branded utopian worlds also fall under this category.

The external world's social influences on the internal consciousness of the consumer affected the ego. In 1923, in *The Ego and the Id*, Freud wrote:

"The ego represents what may be called reason and common sense, in contrast to the id, which contains the passions . . . in its relation to the id is like a man on horseback, who holds in check the superior strength of the horse; the rider tries with his own strength; the ego uses borrowed forces."

The ego allowed the id to realize, and subsequently release, its desires. For marketers this view continued to be held all the way into the twenty-first century. For example, many alcoholic beverages or perfume brands continued to be positioned as conduits which free often young consumers, allowing them to make themselves appear alluring or sophisticated.

It's the first company to build the mental position that has the upper hand, not the first company to make the product. IBM didn't invent the computer; Sperry Rand did. But IBM was the first to build the computer position in the prospect's mind.

Al Ries, author of *Positioning: The battle for your mind*, 1981

In 1981, Al Ries and Jack Trout described how positioning was a marketing communication tool used to reach target customers in a crowded marketplace. They explained that positioning started with a product in a broad market, and the key aim was to position a product in the mind of a particular customer or set of customers.

During the 1990s, soul traders covertly filmed young men chatting up women in nightclubs. The young men proudly clasped bottles of branded beer with the labels pointed outwards. It was argued that this suggested the men were subconsciously saying to the women, "This brand identifies who I am and what I believe in. Date me: enjoy the brand's advertised values and lifestyle."

While the ego exerted rational control over the more rampant id, it didn't guarantee total control. However, when a provocative proposition was positioned in the right light to the id, it offered a degree of acceptable control. Ego could also be swayed by the excitement of the raw id. At this point the super-ego acted like a father figure making sure that passions wouldn't get out of control. To keep things in check and maintain a sense of morality, the super-ego would hand out sentences of guilt, anxiety, and inferiority.

The super-ego instils common sense. Always at odds with the more tolerant ego, it is the aspect of the human psyche that addresses issues such as religion or right and wrong. Serving as an irritant to the defiant id and ego, the super-ego remains the most difficult of soul-trading tactics to employ.

For example, in July 2008, speaking from the Tokyo-hosted G8 meeting of the world's key democracies, British Prime Minister Gordon Brown warned that on average, individual British family units were throwing away food worth £420 ($600) a year. That added up to £1 billion worth of groceries going uneaten annually. The average annual food bill for a family of four went up by £360. Seizing on a marketing opportunity,

British supermarkets temporarily slashed the price of their own-label brand foods by around 75 percent. However, when they compared this to the cachet of eating branded foods, many consumers returned to the more expensive option. A report from the Waste and Resources Action Programme (WRAP) estimated that during 2007–8 British householders threw out 1.3 million unopened yoghurt pots, 5,500 whole chickens, and 440,000 ready meals each day. Such waste was unacceptable in a world facing long-term food crisis. The Prime Minister implored the British public to be more frugal with their weekly food shop. Reporting on the Prime Minister's warning, *The Times* suggested that the public followed some important rules to save on household expenses:

Rule 1: Learn to love your leftovers
Rule 2: Buy seasonal foods
Rule 3: Know and use what's in your store cupboard and your freezer

Staying with the theme, the publisher Collins introduced new words to the British dictionary, including: "recessionista"— a person who dresses down because of the financial crisis; and "brickor mortis"—property that has lost value through the recession.

The response from credit-crunched British consumers was fast and furious. Who was the Prime Minister to give them a lesson in the management of home economics? To make matters worse, within hours of chastizing the general public for their wasteful habits, TV news crews captured the Prime Minister and his seven peers from the other G8 nations tucking into an eight-course meal—much of which was left behind on their gilded plates.

Also in 2008, the British consumer rebelled against the high-street chain Marks & Spencer, long seen as the bellwether of British retail. As part of a general marketing trend for brands to appear green, the high-street stores imposed a five-pence environmental green duty on plastic bags. Coincidently, within three months of introducing the scheme, the company's profits dipped dramatically. The perception of the company being heavily led by quality rather than cost contributed in January 2009 to a 25 percent drop in its share price—the worst for 20 years. Soon afterwards the retailer announced over 1,200 redundancies as well as store closures. While the results were mainly due to horrendous economic conditions, in the media consumers reported that they felt cheated by the previously much-loved company, which already charged a premium on many of its food items.

The heart and soul of the problem lay in the fundamental issue that consumers were used to brands offering a choice of marketing ideals that, while often being socially conscientious, were also selfishly designed to appeal to the id and ego.

Around the same time as Marks & Spencer launched its charge for plastic bags, BMW cars advertised a range of fuel-efficient vehicles which made no compromise on the brand's levels of sophistication and comfort. But even despite offering consumers this environmentally sound choice , a looming global credit crunch saw general car sales slow down to snail's pace. By January 2009 other prestige car brands such as Jaguar announced job losses through record low demand for new vehicles.

You can't always get what you want, but if you try sometimes well you might find, you get what you need
The Rolling Stones, "You Can't Always Get What You Want"

The Marks & Spencer plastic bag case, along with the government's attempted intervention to curb spending, marked a critical point in how marketing was positioned. The world economic situation switched the emphasis of marketing from selling products or services to "demarketing," where brands actually invested money in curbing excessive consumer spending.

Deflation had arrived with a thunderous crash, causing a "credit crunch" that was becoming increasingly uncomfortable. There was an abrupt reduction in easily available loans. In Britain well-established financial brands like the Northern Rock building society went into freefall. On September 14, 2007 the Bank of England had to rescue it from total collapse at the cost of $42 billion.

Over the other side of the pond, by March 2008 the Federal Reserve was forced to inject emergency funding to Bear Stearns, a highly respected wealth management company, which no longer had access to overnight funds. One month later, following a takeover, the Royal Bank of Scotland announced a £12 billion rights issue to rebuild its capital revenues. Things were clearly awry with some of the world's most respected financial institution brands. Yet at the time, judging by the kind of salaries and bonuses still being paid to banking executives, nobody knew that the entire global financial economic system was only three months away from total meltdown.

By the end of July, the German Deutsche Bank reported €5 billion ($7.8 billion) in write-downs in the first half of its second quarter profits. By September the ill wind of the credit crisis was sending a chill down the spine of the global economy. Merrill Lynch caught more than a cold, and was sold at a bargain price of $50 billion to Bank of America. The fallout included over 5,200 job losses. Washington Mutual also fell foul of debts amounting to $19 billion.

American mortgage providers such as Fannie Mae, founded during the Great Depression to purchase mortgages from banks and sell them on to investors, along with Freddie Mac, created in 1970, saw their share values tumbling to catastrophic levels. The sheer dead weight of the crunch caused Fannie Mae and

Freddie Mac to incur debts to the tune of $5.4 trillion. Between them they were involved with over 80 percent of the American housing market. The American government was left to bail them out in what was probably the largest state intervention in the history of the American economy—certainly the largest since the Great Depression.

Within a month of Freddie and Fannie taking their caps in hand to the American government for help, trading levels in New York fell so low that the Dow Jones Industrial Average buckled, pushing it down the steepest decline since the day when the financial markets reopened for business after September 11, 2001.

Night after night the American media reported cases of bankrupt homeowners being accompanied out of their homes by local sheriffs overseeing evictions. In Europe, consumers were warned of impending higher energy bills and lower standards of public service from local authorities that had seen public spending squashed by the credit crunch.

Everybody knows the fight was fixed. The poor stay poor, the rich get rich. That's how it goes. Everybody knows.

Leonard Cohen, "Everybody knows"

The sixth-biggest drop in the Dow Jones Index's history was witnessed on September 15, 2008. Wall Street casualties included the bankruptcy of the world's fourth-biggest bank, the 158-year-old Lehman Brothers' investment bank, which owed $613 billion to creditors in America, Europe and Asia. Barack Obama described the situation as the most serious since the 1930s crash. In London in just one day £50 billion was wiped off the value of leading shares. Job losses continued to rise. Lehman Brothers alone lost 25,000 jobs. Central banks around the world pumped hundreds of billions into global stock markets in a desperate effort to shore up global financial confidence.

After decades of seeing adverts promising fulfilled lives through ownership of the latest must-have item, by 2009 consumers were so deeply addicted to brands that many believed that any reduction of consumerism could leave a shortfall in the enjoyment of life itself. But contrary to the general panic, the world's money didn't disappear overnight. The rich for the most part still remained rich. However, the basic lack of trust between people about extending credit meant that whereas before cash had flowed freely, now there was just a trickle.

Advised by marketers and PR specialists, world politicians powdered their faces for the news cameras and set out to carefully juggle messages of confidence and concern. They pleaded for consumers to start spending rather than give up. Less demand meant less production and would inevitably exacerbate job losses.

With only weeks to leave some kind of positive long-term legacy from his last days in office, President George W. Bush called for a global summit to deal with the monetary disaster. In October 2008, during talks at the Camp David presidential retreat with French President Nicolas Sarkozy and European Commission President José Manuel Barroso, Bush said: "We must resist the dangerous temptation of economic isolationism and continue the policies of open markets that have lifted standards of living and helped millions of people escape poverty around the world."

Captains of industry joined the PR rush, urging businesses not to cut back on advertising. The *Financial Times*, part of the Pearson group, which had seen shares tumble by 17.93 percent between September and October 2008 alone, ran campaigns advocating advertising during a recession. The world's biggest marketing training body made "Marketing in Challenging Times—What Every Business Needs to Know" the theme of its annual conference.

Eventually the situation got so out of hand that many well-known high-street and indeed Wall Street financial brands had to be taken either fully or partially into public ownership. In Iceland, for example, the country's third-largest bank, Glitnir, was bailed out by the Icelandic government at the cost of $864m. Landsbanki, Iceland's second-largest bank, was nationalized, as was Kaupthing, Iceland's largest lender. No fewer than three European governments had to find $16 billion to rescue Fortis, Europe's largest European financial institution. The French bank BNP Paribas took advantage of the situation by taking control of Fortis and buying government assets. The deal made BNP the biggest bank in the Eurozone by deposits.

A wealth of deals followed, such as the one between Santander and the British building society Bradford & Bingley. The Spanish bank purchased the building society's deposit business, leaving the more poorly performing loans side of the organization to the British government, which had been compelled to publicly finance the building society rather than see millions of homeowners left homeless. In time, by funding three of the country's biggest banks to the tune of £37 billion, the British government virtually nationalized the country's entire main banking system.

Reflecting the challenging age of turbulence, in January 2009 Chancellor Alistair Darling announced the biggest government bailout yet for Britain's banks. The government would underwrite "toxic" assets built up by the banks during the credit explosion. However, if companies and individuals defaulted on payments, taxpayers would be exposed to hundreds of billions of pounds in possible losses. Despite the irony of taxpayers (who as homeowners had been sucked into stretching beyond their means) being left to finance the banks, by the first quarter of 2009 up to 300,000 job cuts were expected in Britain's finance sector alone. Building companies laid off workers in their hundreds. Small businesses relying on steady cash flow normally supplemented by banks went out of business.

The entire episode was testimony to the selfishness of the soul traders and the short-term thinking of consumers. Throughout the 1990s and into the first decade of the twenty-first century, ordinary homeowners had been consistently reassured by marketing campaigns that they could and should borrow beyond their means: the prospect of eventual "good times" ahead would even out any immediate shortfalls.

Credit cards became more ubiquitous than cash. Interest-free repayment schemes and freely available loans to even the poorest in society vied with each other to attract customers. Despite a series of commodity crises in sectors such as oil, in the first years of the twenty-first century consumer prices remained restrained. Believing that short-term "busts" would, in time, turn to "booms," everyone continued buying, creating a bubble built on promises.

In America, long-established brand icons such as Ford, General Motors and Chrysler (see Chapter 8) were propped up by the White House throwing them a $17.4 billion emergency lifeline and access to funds previously earmarked for the American government's $700 billion bank rescue plan. In Britain, Woolworths, one of the country's best-loved high-street retailers, was forced to close its 807 stores—just a few months short of celebrating a century of trading. Fatally, Woolworths had relied on its good name alone rather than adapt to changing consumer demands. While many lamented the end of a nostalgic brand, during its last days, rather than worrying about saving the brand, the primary concern of many consumers was simply to buy its last remaining assets at knock-down prices. Many other retailers toppled, leaving thousands jobless. When the bubble burst in 2009 the public realized that many politicians had simply turned a blind eye and dipped an eager hand into the public purse. Now those same politicians were reaching even deeper into the public purse, necessitating the spin doctors to work overtime in order to justify the politicians' actions.

The answer from the spin doctors was to pin much of the blame on a collective Judas. The press were fed stories of financial "fat cat" inflated salaries. Subpoenas relating to malpractice were issued to "greedy" corporate players. The politicians had to clutch on to office and as the public bayed for its pound of flesh, "fat cats" were said to have enjoyed too much cream. Top Cat was Bernard Madoff. He was accused of perpetrating one of the greatest frauds in history by allegedly losing $50 billion of investors' money. His system was based on the Ponzi scheme, a fraudulent pyramid investment operation that pays returns to investors out of the money paid by subsequent investors rather than from profit.

Irrespective of headlines ringing out death tolls for the economy and society, Freud's id and ego were still keen to play if given the chance. For example, writing in the London *Evening Standard*, journalist Lara Craik noted that although consumers were advised to be frugal with their money, thanks to mass marketing, which was still promoting the goal of narrow self-interest, the battle between right and wrong was being won by the wrong side. Switch on virtually any commercial TV channel at this time and it was highly likely that you would catch an ad break featuring celebrities endorsing the L'Oréal make-up brand range. The commercials regularly ended with a celebrity explaining that they chose L'Oréal "because I'm worth it." Commenting on these commercials in *Mail Online*, Craik explained:

"Some things simply can't be compromised: taxis when it's raining . . . food from Waitrose [an upmarket supermarket] because its packaging looks so much nicer in the fridge. My favourite chocolate might cost £3.45 a bar but, by God I'm going to eat it, just as I am going to drink good wine, wear good shoes and book improbably expensive holidays in Ibiza. Why? Not because I can afford it, but because I'm worth it . . . Louise (a friend) earns £11,000 a year—she is always short on her rent but has a fiendish habit for Christian Louboutin shoes at £400 a pop . . . 'Why shouldn't I have that?' we all think, as our Visa bills ratchet up to the sky. 'Because I'm worth it.' It might be the best advertising slogan ever penned."

Although compelling and insistent, the trio of id, ego and super-ego alone can't sustain a brand's positioning in the mind of consumers. Once a brand preference is established it needs to be enforced and ratified by either direct substantiating facts or indirect testimonials. Such endorsements needn't come from experts. Providing they come from people known and respected by consumers, such as TV celebrities, or other consumers, their endorsement won't just be heard, it will be acted upon.

You make your choices then justify why you were right

Quote from *Matrix Revolutions*

The research organization Bright House discovered that if consumers were regularly shown preferred objects the brain's prefrontal cortex (associated with a person's sense of self-worth and esteem) became stimulated. That stimulated a chemical called norepinephrine, implicated in depression.

All this goes a considerable way towards explaining why people are so adamant about protecting their regularly advertised preferred brand choices. Robert B. Cialdini, author of *Influence: Psychology of Persuasion,* noted: "Once we have made a choice or taken a stand, we encounter personal and interpersonal pressures to [retain] that commitment." Believed to come from the School of Management at the Henley Business School, University of Reading, a frequent quote on business courses runs as follows: "Being a consumer today is a full-time job. Never more than a moment away from a purchase opportunity, confronted with an ever more bewildering range of choices, today's consumers are better off, more confused and less predictable than ever." When confronted with a choice between confusion or the reassurance of a trusted brand, the best choice to take becomes clear.

Having been reassured of a brand's validity by various media (called "brand touch points") such as the web, press, TV, and public relations, consumers can resist even the most persuasive of campaigns designed to show a brand in a negative light. Such negative challenges to the brand become a direct challenge to the customer's ego and choice. This relates to a state of mind called "cognitive dissonance," in which people will justify their choices, despite any evidence suggesting that it might be a poor decision.

Robert Cialdini suggested six "weapons of influence," all of which could be used by soul traders:

Reciprocation People feel obliged to return favors. To take advantage of this weapon, soul traders may advertise free product samples.

Commitment and consistency Once committed verbally or in writing to an idea or goal, there is a greater chance that people will honor a promise. In direct marketing, the earlier and longer you can convince a consumer to pledge to a brand, the more awkward it becomes for them to renege on that promise. In sales, once a buyer is committed to a purchase, often, even if suddenly the price is raised at the last moment, the sale will remain secure.

Social proof Individuals follow people. People follow herds. Herds follow crowds. For example, if for no obvious reason someone gazes into the sky, passing bystanders often look up to see what's there. Once two bystanders stop and stare, three join in and so on until someone realizes that there is nothing to actually see—at which point two . . . three . . . six . . . also come to the same conclusion, and so walk on.

Authority People tend to obey authority figures, especially those in a uniform, even when asked to perform objectionable acts.

Cialdini cited the Milgram experiments in the 1960s in which people acted against their own conscience and inflicted pain on others, providing that an authority figure had assured them that it was appropriate to do so. The My Lai massacre, when American servicemen murdered hundreds of Vietnamese civilians, is another example of obedience to authority.

Liking Friendly and approachable peers also influence people. That's one reason why TV and radio producers often choose casual-looking actors with easy-going voices to sell goods or services.

Scarcity Perceived scarcity generates demand. For example, saying offers are available for a "limited time only" encourages sales.

In copywriting, soul traders often lace copy with compelling reasons for why a brand is a perfect personal choice. To make those reasons even more persuasive, a storyline relating to the consumer's own experience ensures people feel involved with a brand ideal.

I hope I'm not a tourist attraction
Prince William

One brand wishing to come across as being "the people's choice" is the British royal family. In 2008 I was invited to talk to Sky News about Prince William's brand. The news channel wanted to know if the Prince's brand was being manipulated to sway waning support for royalty. I explained that those who were loyal to the royal family would seek out media stories validating their choice to remain steadfast in their support. Spin doctors devising such stories had to show the royal family as being consistent, even during bad times, and relevant to the public—in Britain and the Commonwealth as well as beyond.

Consistency meant reassuring the public that royal heritage was being passed on to a safe pair of hands. On discussing the public's allegiance to the royal family, Her Majesty Queen Elizabeth II once noted, "People like continuity and consistency." Relevancy was marketed by showing images of Prince William and his brother Prince Harry doing things that young men (albeit in their cases, very privileged young men) would be likely to do. Together, "consistency" and "relevance" demonstrated an ongoing story of leadership.

> *A leader is one who knows the way, goes the way and shows the way*
>
> John C. Maxwell, author, speaker and "leadership" expert

As in the twenty-first century, back in the 1940s the psychology of leadership, choice and civic duty was of paramount importance to brands. In America, the war meant people enduring rationed goods and services. A young copywriter called Nelson Metcalf perceptively recognized that the nation's hardship could become a focal point to present American services as a source of pride.

At the time Metcalf worked for the New Haven Railroad. In 1944 he wrote an advert called "The Kid in Upper 4," which became so popular that it was turned into a song and even endorsed by rival rail companies. It went like this:

"The Kid in Upper 4.

It is 3:42 am on a troop train. Men wrapped in blankets are breathing heavily. Two in every lower berth. One in every upper. This is no ordinary trip. It may be their last in America until the end of the war. Tomorrow they will be on the high seas. One is wide-awake, listening, staring into the blackness.

It is the kid in Upper 4.

Tonight, he knows, he is leaving behind a lot of little things—and big ones.

The taste of hamburgers and pop . . . the feel of driving a roadster over a six-lane highway . . . a dog named Shucks, or Spot, or Barnacle Bill.

The pretty girl who writes so often . . . that gray-haired man, so proud and awkward at the station . . . the mother who knit the socks he'll wear soon.

Tonight he's thinking them over. There's a lump in his throat. And maybe—a tear fills his eye. It doesn't matter kid. Nobody will see . . . it's too dark.

A couple of thousand miles away, where he's going, they don't know him very well. But people all over the world are waiting, praying for him to come.

And he will come, this kid in Upper 4.

With new hope, peace and freedom for a tired, bleeding world. Next time you are on the train, remember the kid in Upper 4.

If you have to stand en route—it is so he may have a seat. If there is no berth for you—it is so that he may sleep. If you have to wait for a seat in the diner—it is so he . . . and thousands like him . . . may have a meal they won't forget in the days to come. For to treat him as our most honored guest is the least we can do to pay a mighty debt of gratitude. The New Haven R.R."

Other brands to jump on the World War II propaganda bandwagon included Lucky Strike, issued to the American GIs as part of their regular rations. In 1942 Lucky Strike sponsored radio programs with jingles such as "Lucky Strike Green has gone to war," a reference to the green dye on Lucky Strike's cartons, exclusively designed for the military. Other packs were changed to white with red and black—still featured on Lucky Strike packaging.

With the men going to war, women had to keep the home front going in both Britain and America. The US Office of War

Information coordinated a propaganda program featuring a headscarf-wearing woman called "Rosie the Riveter," based on Rose Monroe who worked at an aircraft plant in Michigan. The poster showing Rosie flexing her muscles had a headline reading "We can do it!" The campaign was meant to inspire women to fulfill their patriotic duties by "doing the job he left behind."

Initially only single women were targeted. Married women were thought to already have more than enough on their plates as mothers. However, as the war went on, even married women were recruited to pitch in. From a pre-war figure of 12 million American women employed, the number rose to 20 million, taking in jobs like factory work, mail delivery, air traffic control and of course riveting—all previously jobs held by men.

8

Marketing on the
Coke side of life

*The goal of modern propaganda is no
longer to transform opinion but to arouse
an active and mythical belief*

Jacques Ellul, philosopher

Coca-Cola epitomizes the story of brands and propaganda. More than a drink it is a taste of nostalgia for a time that perhaps never existed and a figment of the collective imagination. It is a brand is so steeped in mythology, legends and hearsay that an alien visiting planet Earth could easily mistake our obsession with it as devotion to some kind of cult religion.

So crucial is the Coca-Cola brand to all marketers that here we can rest from our journey back and forth in history, pull a tab, take a sip, and consider the unspoken side of the story of one of the few brands in the world that like jeans, is classless and all-pervasive.

The history of Coca-Cola is the often funny story of a group of men obsessed with putting a trivial soft drink "within an arm's reach of desire."

Mark Pendergrast, *For God, Country, and Coca-Cola*

It was a chemist, John Smith Pemberton, serving in the first state-run facility to test soil and crop chemicals, who created Coca-Cola. The drink was originally sold as a coca-wine, called Pemberton's French Wine Coca (1885). The beverage could be drunk as an alternative to alcoholic wine, at the time prohibited in America. According to some reports the drink was named "Coca-Cola" because its syrup contained a derivative stimulant from coca leaves, from which cocaine is produced. Some alleged that this amounted to a dose of 8.46 mg of cocaine. Kola nuts gave the beverage flavor and caffeine. The original ingredients included five ounces of coca leaf per gallon of syrup (although later some disputed the precise amount). By 1904, the same year the American hamburger was introduced at the Louisiana Purchase Exhibition in St Louis, Missouri, Coca-Cola started using the leftovers of the cocaine extraction process that left only minuscule traces of potent cocaine in the drink. Today the company includes a completely non-narcotic coca leaf extract. In 2008 Coca-Cola ran an advertising campaign pointing out that, ever since 1886, the drink had never contained added preservatives or artificial flavors. On its website the company proudly declares, "No added preservatives or artificial flavors. Never had. Never will. The real thing since 1886."

The kosher recipe

The complete official list of ingredients is still known by only a limited number of people. One is a rabbi who needs to ensure that the drink is kosher. (In 1935 Rabbi Tobias Greffen became the first rabbi to be told the secret ingredients.) The most mysterious ingredients in the actual brew include items known only as 7X and Merchandise #5. In India manufacturers are obliged by law to say what is in a drink. Rather than reveal the secret ingredients, in 1977 the company decided to suspend marketing Coca-Cola in India.

Back in the nineteenth century, Pemberton marketed the drink as a patent medicine, which he claimed could cure many ailments including neurasthenia and dyspepsia. (Caleb D. Bradham marketed his own elixir for the latter—"Pepsi"—in 1898.) Pemberton even claimed that Coca-Cola could offer relief from morphine addiction.

The distinctive logo was designed in 1885 by Pemberton's bookkeeper, Frank Mason Robinson. The typeface became the font of choice in America during the nineteenth century. The first advertisement for Coca-Cola ran in 1888, but in the first eight months only nine drinks were sold each day.

Reportedly under the influence of morphine, Pemberton sold the rights to the drink no fewer than three times over. In 1887, Asa Griggs Candler attained a stake in Pemberton's company. Candler soon incorporated it as the Coca-Cola Company. However, Pemberton had also sold the rights to J. C. Mayfield,

A. O. Murphey, C. O. Mullagy and E. H. Bloodworth. To confuse issues further still, Pemberton's alcoholic son, Charley, also sold a version of the drink.

In the summer of 1888, Candler was compelled to sell the drink under the brand names "Yum Yum" and "Koke." Neither name caught on. Candler was forced to obtain exclusive rights. Yet even this plan was spoilt when in 1914 one of the signatories on the sale, Margaret Dozier, claimed her signature was forged—as was Pemberton's.[2] Pemberton passed away on August 16, 1888 and his beverage went on to become one of the world's most pervasive brands. Advertising agencies D'Arcy St Louis and Massengale, based in Atlanta, were the first (*c.*1906) to produce large-scale newspaper advertising for the company. They started with what at the time were considered to be especially provocative adverts, featuring a buxom waitress called Juanita.

D'Arcy remained Coca-Cola's agency for 50 years. Arthur "Archie" Lee, the creative chief at D'Arcy, oversaw the account, creating slogans for Coca-Cola such as "the pause that refreshes." D'Arcy's own original logo featured an arrow through a letter "D." D'Arcy fully exploited the self-publicity monogram in its Coca-Cola adverts—paid for by the client—running the slogan: "Whenever you see an arrow, think of Coca-Cola."

Not all future Coca-Cola slogans would turn out successful. Coca Cola first launched in China as "ke-kou-ke-la." This unexpectedly translated as: "bite the wax tadpole" or "horse stuffed with wax." Coca-Cola eventually marketed its Chinese product under a different slogan, which, although sounding very different to the usual Coca-Cola branding message, had a greater local appeal: "Can mouth, can happy."

In Dutch, the slogan "Refresh Yourself With Coca-Cola" meant "Wash Your Hands With Coca-Cola." In Cuba, the soft-drink manufacturer tested skywriting its slogan: "Tome Coca-Cola" (Drink Coca-Cola). A sudden shift in wind direction caused the skywriting to change shape. The crowds below saw the message as "Teme Coca-Cola" (Fear Coca-Cola). In France, "Have a Coke and a Smile," when heard as lyrics in a song, was often misunderstood as "Have a Coke and a Mouse."

As for Pepsi, the advertising slogan "Come alive with the Pepsi generation" was translated into Chinese as, "Pepsi will bring your ancestors back from the dead."

Santa—the real thing?

In 1862, during the American Civil War, the cartoonist Thomas Nast drew Santa Claus for *Harper's Weekly*. Santa was depicted as a small elf-like figure who supported the Union. By good chance for the Coca-Cola Company, the character wore red and white—inadvertently reflecting the company's brand colors. Officially the company explains the red suit came from Nast's interpretation of St Nick.

In the 1920s, the Coca-Cola Company began its Christmas advertising with shopping-related ads in magazines like the *Saturday Evening Post*. At this time, consumers drank Coca-Cola mainly when the weather was hot. In 1922 the Coca-Cola Company started a campaign "Thirst Knows No Season," and continued with a campaign again connecting the brand to Santa Claus.

In 1930, artist Fred Mizen painted a department-store Santa in a crowd drinking a bottle of Coke. In 1931, the Coca-Cola Company commissioned Michigan-born illustrator Haddon Sundblom to develop advertising images showing Santa himself rather than just a man dressed as "Santa," as Mizen's work had portrayed him. Sundblom was inspired by Clement Clark Moore's 1822 poem "A Visit From St Nicholas" (commonly known as "Twas the Night Before Christmas"). Sundblom's Santa was said to be based on a live model—his friend Lou Prentiss—a retired salesman. When Prentiss died, Sundblom used himself as a model, painting while looking into a mirror.

1930 was also the year when radio listeners could tune in to one of the first national coast-to-coast radio programs, "The Coca-Cola Hour," broadcast nightly on NBC. The show was a mix of celebrity interviews, sports news and live music played by the 31-piece Coca-Cola Dance Orchestra. Leonard Joy, the conductor, composed a simple theme tune for the program, "Coca-Cola Signature." The tune, which was preceded by the sound of a bottle of Coca-Cola being opened, was the company's first official jingle and was used for over two decades.

The Coca-Cola Santa made its official debut in 1931 in the *Saturday Evening Post* and appeared regularly in that magazine, as well as in *Ladies Home Journal, National Geographic*, the *New Yorker* and others. From 1931–64, Coca-Cola advertising showed Santa enjoying a Coke, playing with children who stayed up to greet him and raiding the refrigerators at a number of homes.

Have a Coca-Cola = Howdy neighbor . . . or greeting friends at home or abroad
World War II Coca-Cola advertisement

By World War II, Coca-Cola was far more than just a beverage. It was marketed on the basis that it was as "genuine" and "good-natured" as Father Christmas himself. That made it the perfect refreshment for serving American GIs, offering them a taste of "home away from home." Starting in 1939 with only five overseas bottling plants, by 1945 Coca-Cola had 64. At the height of World War II, General Dwight D. Eisenhower sent GIs around six bottles every six months. By the time the last shot was fired in 1945, around five million bottles of Coca-Cola had been drunk.

What was good for the American GIs was also good for the German SS, who were in need of a drink that tasted better than the local water supply, which needed sterilizing with chlorine. At the start of the war, under the leadership of CEO Max Keith,

Coca-Cola GmbH (Germany) happily collaborated with Hitler's administration to build bottling plants in occupied territories. According to Mark Pendergrast, the author of *For God, Country, and Coca Cola*, Coke used forced labor in the bottling plants. Describing a 1,500-strong business convention held during March 1938, presided over by Max Keith, the University of Virginia's educational resource website notes that behind the main table a huge banner declared in German, "Coca-Cola is the world-famous trademark for the unique product of the Coca-Cola GmbH." Directly below were three huge red, white, and black swastikas. Rallying his workers, Keith said, "We will reach our goal only if we muster all our power in a total effort. Our marvellous drink has the power of endurance to continue this march to success." The meeting closed with a resounding, threefold "Sieg Heil" to Hitler.

Maintaining the company's traditional ties to the Olympic Games, the German division of Coke even sponsored the 1936 Olympics. Coke's association with the Nazis was so strong that invariably, whenever a local magazine featured the Führer's picture on the front, Coca-Cola GmbH would advertise on the back. Advertising included billboards around the Olympic stadiums in Berlin offering a backdrop to troops of parading Nazis.

According to reports, an advert in the October 1938 issue of the army magazine *Die Wehrmacht* showed a hand holding out a Coke bottle in front of a world map underlined by the caption "*Ja, Coca-Cola hat Weltruf*" (Yes, Coca-Cola enjoys an international reputation). The advertising's copy stated, "Of the forty million automobilists from all over the world increasing attention is demanded, which is the reason why they 'like to take advantage of the 'pause that refreshes'."

The Jewish question

Not everyone in Nazi Germany approved of Coca-Cola. In 1936 a competing drinks manufacturer, Afri-Cola, published flyers featuring Coca-Cola bottle caps from America with Hebrew inscriptions. The inscriptions indicated that Coke was kosher. According to Afri-Cola this suggested that Coca-Cola was a Jewish company. Nazi Party headquarters hastily cancelled their orders for Coca-Cola.

In an attempt to secure orders and appease the Nazis, Coca-Cola placed ads in *Der Stürmer* denouncing the accusations. The official Nazi publication was renowned for its twisted anti-Semitism. The ads did not go unnoticed in America and produced angry headlines claiming "Coca-Cola finances Hitler."

In 1939, the Ministry of Economics demanded that Coca-Cola bottles conform to a metric standard based on decimals. The Coke bottle contained 180 cubic centimeters instead of the requisite 200. Pointing to this anomaly the Nazis stopped the production of new bottles, ignoring the fact that a larger bottle would have had severe consequences for Germany's paltry supply of glass.

Coca-Cola dealt with this by moving production to the recently annexed Sudetenland, where German laws, including packaging regulations, didn't fully apply. What was good for business was equally good for the Nazi government, which was able to dodge an international embargo designed to cripple it.

Hitler's choice

By 1941, the company could no longer import the essential syrup containing 7X and Merchandise #5 from America. Enterprising as ever, the company invented a new drink—this time especially for the Nazis, called "Fanta." The name was chosen in a contest run by Max Keith in which workers were asked to express their "Fantasie" (German for "fantasy"). Joe Knipp, a salesperson, shouted out, "Fanta!"

At first Fanta contained whey, a by-product of cheese, and apple fibre, but ingredients varied throughout the war. In 1943 alone, over three million bottles of Fanta were sold in Nazi Germany. Coca-Cola officially acquired the company in 1960. After the war, the Coca-Cola American icon grew even stronger. Eventually, so-called "Coca-Colanization" saw the brand bottled throughout every corner of the world. In 1966 the American people questioned why Cyprus, a country with a tiny population compared to Israel, was offered a bottling franchise, whereas the only democratic state in the Middle East wasn't. In response, and with the support of America, Coca-Cola ignored a boycott made by the Arab League and started to do business with Israel. The Arab League subsequently boycotted Coca-Cola from August 1968 to May 1991—except for Egypt, which dealt with the company from 1979.

Pepsi also used the excuse of Israel being too small for a franchise, but they concentrated their marketing efforts on conquering the richer Arab states. That created a loss of goodwill with many American consumers, who maintained that the company was anti-Israel.

Pepsi's eventual entry into Israel in 1992 got off to a false start with an ill-conceived advertising campaign featuring the evolution of a monkey into a Pepsi drinker. This offended Israel's religious community, as did the arrival of Michael Jackson who endorsed the brand, and who landed in Israel on the Jewish Sabbath (when travel by mechanised transport is not allowed).

Today, reflecting a belief in profits before prophets, both Coca-Cola and Pepsi are widely available throughout the Middle East. Coca-Cola has more than 450 different sparkling and still brands in over 200 countries. PepsiCo has become a world leader in convenience snacks, foods and beverages, with 2008 revenues of more than $39 billion and over 185,000 employees.

9

Profits of war

War is a racket. It always has been. It is possibly the oldest, easily the most profitable, surely the most vicious. It is the only one international in scope. It is the only one in which the profits are reckoned in dollars and the losses in lives.

Major General Smedley D. Butler, two-time Congressional
Medal of Honor Recipient, US Marine Corps

This exploration through the annals of history proves beyond doubt that for soul traders, war can turn a healthy profit. From World War II to the wars in Iraq and Afghanistan, for those brave brands willing to put their logo where a bullet strikes, appalling losses on the battlefield can lead to the creation of fortunes in the ledger book.

General Motors is a great car and truck manufacturer with a long history of outstanding corporate citizenship. At GM, corporate responsibility is more than words. It is an acknowledgment that our actions shape our reputation.

Rod Gillum, *VP Corporate Responsibility and Diversity*, from GM website

Coca-Cola wasn't alone in profiting from Nazi Germany. From 1920, General Motors (GM), part of the vast Du Pont Family interests, was in charge of Adam Opel AG, a German automobile manufacturer. In 1937 the company was changed into an armaments operation producing items like the Opel Blitz 3-ton trucks, as well as aircraft components and engines, land mines, and torpedo detonators.

Almost 17 percent of Opel's Blitz trucks were sold directly to the Nazi military. By 1938, sales of trucks to the Nazis increased to 29 percent, totalling about 6,000 Blitz trucks that year alone. GM's Opel business was so brisk that by 1939 the company was one of Germany's biggest employers, employing 27,000 people. Big money led to an urgent need to cover up Opel's link to its American owners. Beginning in 1934, the company ensured that its directors included Nazi Party members.

Around 1935, GM ensured that Opel Germany had the technology to produce the modern gasoline additive tetraethyl lead, commonly called "ethyl" or leaded gasoline. So thanks in part to American leadership, the Reich's Opel vehicles became more fuel-efficient. After the war, the "First Architect of the Reich," Albert Speer, told a congressional investigator that Germany could not have attempted its September 1939 blitzkrieg on Poland without the performance-boosting additive from Opel.

Alfred Sloan Jr., Chairman of GM, said in 1939 that the company's German subsidiaries were "highly profitable" and that Germany's internal political affairs "should not be considered the business of the management of General Motors."[3] While making money from the Third Reich, from 1941–5 GM also reaped the rewards of building and operating around $900 million worth of defence manufacturing facilities for the Allies. Commenting on GM's profits, American Secretary of War Henry Stimson later explained that when a capitalist country wages war, "you have to let business make money out of the process, or business won't work."

By the end of the war, GM reclaimed central control over Opel operations and because the Allies had bombed its German facilities, GM collected around $33 million in "war reparations."

In 1953, GM President Charlie Wilson was nominated Secretary of Defense. He was asked if he could make a decision in the country's interest that was contrary to GM's interest. Wilson replied, "I cannot conceive of one, because for years I thought what was good for our country was good for General Motors, and vice versa. The difference did not exist. Our company is too big." (Following the global credit crunch at the start of the twenty-first century, the American Treasury unveiled a $6 billion rescue package for GMAC—General Motors' troubled car loan arm, by then co-owned by Chrysler's owner, Cerberus.)

According to Edwin Black, author of *IBM and the Holocaust*, the famous computing company also had dealings with the Third Reich. Hitler turned to IBM to streamline the technical running of their death and slave-labor camps. IBM provided the regime with "Hollerith tabulation" machines that used punch cards to perform calculations in concentration camps. Black said: "The head office in New York had a complete understanding of everything that was going on in the Third Reich with its machines . . . that their machines were being used in concentration camps generally, and that they knew Jews were being exterminated."

The management consultant Peter Drucker recalls how he once discussed the situation with the then head of IBM, Thomas Watson, who had strong reservations about dealing with the Nazis, not out of any issues of morality, but "because Watson, with a very keen sense of public relations, thought it was risky from a business perspective."

He who profits by a crime commits it.

Seneca, Roman philosopher

American corporate profiteering didn't stop with the end of World War II. War historian Stuart Brandes suggests that each new war is infected with new forms of war profiteering. The website Alternet.org listed a top ten of companies profiting from the Iraq War at the start of the twenty-first century.

Towards the end of 2000, around 48,000 American private security and military contractors (PMCs) were stationed in Iraq. In early 2005, CIA officials told the *Washington Post* that at least 50 percent of its estimated $40 billion budget for that year would go to private contractors.

Twenty miles west of Baghdad, the Abu Ghraib prison was commandeered by the coalition forces and used by service personnel to sodomize and torture Iraqis. According to Alternet.org, during the war brand leader CACI (formerly California Analysis Center, Inc.) provided a total of 36 interrogators in Iraq, including up to ten at Abu Ghraib at any one time. Another company, Titan, provided services such as translators. CACI and Titan's involvement at Abu Ghraib prompted the Center for Constitutional Rights to pursue companies and their employees in American courts. "We believe that CACI and Titan engaged in a conspiracy to torture and abuse detainees, and did so to make more money," said Susan Burke, an attorney hired by the Center for Constitutional Rights (CCR), whose lawsuit against the companies is (at the time of writing) proceeding before the Federal Court for the District of Columbia.

Alternet.org explains that in September 2005, CACI announced that it would no longer do interrogation work in Iraq. Early in the same year, Titan pleaded guilty to three international bribery charges and agreed to pay a record $28.5 million penalty in compliance with the Foreign Corrupt Practices Act. The company's contract with the US Army was extended and according to the website, at the time of writing, is currently worth over $1 billion. The San Francisco-based construction and engineering giant received a no-bid contract worth $2.4 billion to help coordinate and rebuild a large part of Iraq's infrastructure. However, according to the website, much of the work was either not completed or fell below industry standard quality. Aegis, a security firm based in Britain, allegedly won a $293 million contract in Iraq, despite the fact that American competitors had submitted lower bids.

Custer Battles became the first Iraq occupation contractor to be found guilty of fraud. A jury ordered the company to pay more than $10 million in damages for 37 counts of fraud, including false billing. Later an American judge in the case dismissed the majority of the charges on a technicality. General Dynamics supplied the American Army with everything from bullets to tank shells to Stryker vehicles. American newspapers report that since 9/11 the company's profits have tripled. Nour USA received $400 million in Iraq contracts, including an $80 million contract to provide oil pipeline security. Some critics at the time of Nour's bid for the work pointed out that the company had no previous related experience.[4]

10

Brands are a many-splendored thing

Oh yes, I'm the great pretender.

The Platters, "The Great Pretender" (1955)

The 1880s introduced branding on ranches, but it was not until the 1950s that the world witnessed the birth of a modern version of branding consumers. But thanks to the invention of TV, for the first time companies could deliver their messages directly into the homes of consumers, branding consumers as effectively as the cowboys had branded their cattle.

The decade saw brands position themselves as close family friends. Unregulated cigarette manufacturers "pushed" their wares specifically at children. Gas-guzzling cars were aimed at dads. In America, moms struggling to balance household chores were offered the dream of being treated as queens. Today, fashions and tone of voice may have changed, but the message of fulfilment through brands remains uncannily familiar.

On evenings speckled with stars, at drive-in movie theatres like the one just off Route 48 Minetto, New York, 1950s teenagers would test their luck by putting their arm around their girlfriend as they sipped on their Coca-Colas. One such teenager, Dwayne, and his "gal" Kellie sat in the front seat of an electric blue Oldsmobile Rocket 88 Convertible. Kellie touched up her make-up by Maybelline. The brand had just received a much welcomed publicity shot in the arm by becoming the title of Chuck Berry's latest hit song, "Maybelline." Clinging to each other, the couple watched Glenn Ford in *Blackboard Jungle*, as he desperately tried to control a class of unruly students. Unfolding his arms, Dwayne dipped into his top pocket and tapped out a brown-filtered Marlboro. Placing it on Kellie's lips he drew out a second one for himself. Striking his match he lit his cigarette and used the glowing embers to kindle Kellie's own stick perched between her painted flaming-red lips. This was cloud-nine smoky heaven; the all-American dream with the lovely gal by his side.

Dwayne's flip-top packet of Marlboro cigarettes had been more than rebranded; it had undergone an entire sex change performed by advertising agency Leo Burnett. No longer was the brand a woman's cigarette, as it had been back in 1924 when it was advertised as being, "As mild as May." Now it was the definitive smoke of the macho male. To seal the deal, a commercial was made showing a chain-smoking man in a checked shirt fixing his pride and joy automobile, whilst recommending Marlboro. Supporting adverts of a baby in its cot were also published, with the caption from the baby reading: "I should say not! My dad would never smoke anything but a Marlboro."

By the mid-1950s an even more rugged cowboy version of the Marlboro man rode his trusty steed into town. Puffing on his cigarette and urging smokers to "Come to Marlboro country," he was to become the icon of an era. Years later the highly respected advertising magazine *AdAge* selected the Marlboro man as the most powerful brand image of the twentieth century.

A B-movie actor, William Thourlby, first played the cowboy. Subsequent Marlboro men included sportsmen like Charley Conerly and Jim Patton of the New York Giants. There was even a European version of the Marlboro cowboy—played by George Lazenby—who went on to play James Bond in *On Her Majesty's Secret Service*, but the two best-known Marlboro cowboys were Wayne McLaren and David Millar.

As each lugged down another lungful of pure Marlboro Country smoke, their broody looks became synonymous with clean open-air living. Within a few short years millions of starry-eyed teenagers around the globe, like Dwayne and Kellie, ensured that a packet of the red-roofed Marlboros were always on hand for a good night out.

It never occurred to any of them that cigarettes could kill. After all, since the 1940s the Camel cigarette brand had claimed, "More doctors smoke Camels than any other cigarette." This was based on a 1947 survey commissioned by Camel of more than 100,000 physicians. In another Camel advertisement, the company encouraged smokers to get hooked on the cigarettes by giving themselves time to get used to the taste:

> "The thorough test of any cigarette is steady smoking. Smoke only Camels for the next 30 days . . . And see how mild Camels are, pack after pack . . . how well they agree with your throat as you steadily smoke. See if you don't find Camel more enjoyable than any other cigarette you've ever smoked."

In the 1950s, American brands like Lucky Strike and Chesterfield accounted for more than 80 percent of all local cigarette sales. Advertisers claimed that advertising was not aimed at encouraging smoking but tempting existing smokers to switch brands. To this end, slogans were produced including: "Not a cough in a carload" (Chesterfield); "Not a single case of throat irritation due to smoking Camels" (Camel); "Cause no ills" (Chesterfield); and "Smoking's more fun when you are not worried by throat irritation or smoker's cough" (Philip Morris).

Inevitably, the Marlboro cowboys, McLaren and Millar, died from emphysema, rather than just old age. As rumors circulated about health hazards and tobacco, during the 1950s the tobacco industry turned to John Wiley Hill's public relations company to downplay emerging evidence linking cancer and other health issues to cigarettes. Hill set up "independent" groups, such as the Tobacco Industry Research Committee (TIRC) founded by Philip Morris, which just happened to own the Marlboro brand. The committees aimed to uncover alternative reasons why tobacco smokers frequently suffered from lung cancer. Vast sums were spent on marketing and very little on actual scientific research. According to a 1972 Council for Tobacco Research

(CTR) industry memo, "The Roper Proposal," written by Fred Panzer, the Committee actually worked at "promoting cigarettes and protecting them from these and other attacks" by "creating doubt about the health charge without actually denying it, and advocating the public's right to smoke, without actually urging them to take up the practice."[5]

Judge H. Lee Sarokin, who presided over two New Jersey tobacco cases, described TIRC/CTR in 1988 as "nothing but a hoax created for public relations purposes with no intention of seeking the truth or publishing it." In 1993, the *Wall Street Journal* described CTR's work as "the longest-running misinformation campaign in American business history."

The Marlboro cowboys wouldn't turn out to be the last characters specifically designed to get the young hooked on cigarettes—that particular accolade was reserved for another "Joe" who would make his debut in the 1980s. Another brand of the 1950s offered to sort out any telltale signs of smoking with the slogan, "You'll wonder where the yellow went when you brush your teeth with Pepsodent."

The suave-talking character played by Alan Ladd in *Branded*, along with the Marlboro man, had yet another connection with the darker side of marketing's ongoing evolution. Both paid homage to a period in American history that shared the consequences of many over-hyped and over-marketed concepts—the American Wild West.

While movies like *Branded* suggested that the Wild West must have endured for at least half a century, in reality the era only lasted between the years 1866 and 1886. American cowboys would brand their cattle to warn people who the rancher was and so prevent them from staking any claim to the herd. This gave rise to the modern notion of "branding," with the key difference that it encouraged people to "put their hands on" the brand rather than keep their hands off it.

The National Cowboy Hall of Fame and Western Heritage Museum in Oklahoma City describes the original branding process as follows:

> "Ketch Hands roped each calf and pulled it near the branding fire. Flankers then grabbed the calf by the ear and loose skin of the flank . . . and the appropriate branding iron was brought to the fire. While one man held the calf, an Iron Man branded it at the hips, ribs or shoulder according to the practice of the owner. Iron Tenders heated the irons in the coals of wood or cow chip fire until the iron turned the color of the ashes—not red hot. If the iron was too hot it caused a sore that could become infected. Too cold, the mark would 'hair-over' and leave no lasting brand impact."

In modern branding the equivalent job of the ropers who targeted the cattle is done by database managers and list brokers. The task of drawing buyers towards the branding fire falls to pre-purchase activities such as web marketing, viral marketing and awareness advertising. Advertising executives who ensure that creative work is appropriate for the target audience replace Iron Tenders. The Iron Man is the brand director, who ensures a campaign has a lasting effect on consumers without it becoming too irritating.

Our models can beat up their models
Levi's® advertising slogan

On May 20, 1873, Levi Strauss and his business partner, a tailor called David Jacobs, received American patent No. 139121 for their blue jeans trousers made from French twilled cotton cloth called "serge de Nîmes" (hence "denim").

In 1890 Levi Strauss's waist overall, known as the "XX," was given the factory lot number 501®. The 501, originally produced for prospectors in the California Gold Rush, became a best-seller with cowboys. The Levi's® two-horse brand design was first used in 1886. In 1936, to further brand the jeans, a red tab was added to the left rear pocket.

With the advent of 1950s media such as TV, branding took on an entirely new dimension. Rather than warning consumers not to touch what wasn't theirs, by the rock 'n' roll decade, brand logos gave consumers the green light to lay their hands all over products and services.

Bright young advertising men like David Ogilvy stepped onto the marketing stage. By the start of the 1950s, Ogilvy's agency had been established for some two years. He realized that the ideal people to aim advertisements at were no longer just the male heads of households but consumers he called "Rosies," who controlled the purse strings. "The consumer is not a moron, she is your wife," he warned. Ogilvy restlessly championed the consumer's intelligence and right to more relevant information rather than platitudes: "What really decides consumers to buy or not to buy is the content of your advertising, not its form." Such consumers deserved the latest, greatest and best-made propositions the marketing people could dream up and substantiate.

The watchword for commercials was "new," closely followed by "faster" or "better." Fast-paced rock 'n' roll spurred on Fast Moving Consumer Goods (FMCG), like washing powder, soap and chocolates. Children were encouraged to buy toothpastes such as IPana. The brand's 1950s TV commercial showed a cartoon character called Bucky Beaver singing:

"New Ipana knocks out decay germs best of all leading brands . . . Brusha-Brusha-Brusha, here's the new IPana with the brand new flavor. It's Dandy For Your Teeth!"

Teenagers seeking to impress on a date were marketed products such as Helene Curtis' Spray Net, whose 1959 commercial promised to preserve "all the joy of naturally curly hair." Fastidious parents were sold practical products like Scotties tissue paper—not to blow noses but to clean car windows, touch up make-up or wipe ice cream off messy children's cheeks. Families, rebuilding their homes after the war, were enticed into buying so-called "white goods," appliances like washing machines and fridges, as well as "brown goods" like furniture.

One commercial for Hoover featured a barbershop trio singing their praises for the new Hoover vacuum cleaner, to the tune of "Oh my darling Clementine":

"In the carpet, in the carpet,
Excavating through the pile.
Works a pit gang called the grit gang,
Digging deeper all the while.
Oh my carpet, oh my carpet, oh my carpet don't forget.
With a Hoover, yes a Hoover, we will beat the blighters yet."

Another typical commercial of the time eavesdropped on a group of housewives discussing the emancipation of American women. One housewife pointed to the importance of women's right to vote: "Carol, you sweet dumb thing, pull up your flaps, you're dragin'." But Carol realizes that real emancipation has come about through her new Whirlpool washing machine, which has meant: " . . . no more clothes lines, no more dark basements, no more blue Monday, here's real emancipation any woman can have . . . ."

As children throughout America brushed their teeth along with Bucky the Beaver, one 'mom', Ruth Handler, was working with Mattel Creations to launch a doll aimed at pre-teenage girls. Based on a German novelty doll called Lilli, it went on to symbolize young womanhood for generations of girls throughout the world.

By the beginning of the twenty-first century billions of Barbies had been sold. By then, though, the doll was thought to be too traditional, and was usurped by the more street-cred Bratz range.

As the 1950s progressed, it was time for brands to evolve once again. From being marketed in the early 1900s as feature-led products and services, to the 1930s when marketing concentrated on the practical uses of a product, by the 1950s brands had become all about experiences and how they made consumers feel about themselves.

Brands didn't just affect the West. In China, the artist Zhang Zhenshi painted what was to become an iconic image of Chairman Mao's bust beaming from a red background—shedding his aura on the people. Despite the radically different social system, these too were images still very much focused on shaping experiences and feelings.

Soul traders had constructed a romantic world where consumers felt positive about rebuilding shattered lives following World War II. With the key to their happiness coming from even more products to add to their clean tissues, perfectly figured dolls and immaculately coiffured hair.

Advertisers competed as sponsors of TV programs pumped directly into consumers' homes. Programs such as *Queen for the Day*, which was originally broadcast on radio, offered hard-done-by ordinary women the chance to assert themselves—at least for a day. Such "benevolence" appealed to brands wishing to have their products or services associated with the notion of being the key to opening doors to newly improved lives.

Another admired TV program, *Strike it Rich*, offered impoverished families the chance to win cash prizes for causes such as medical treatment. If they didn't win any money they could still appeal to a special "Heart Line" where viewers wishing to donate to the contestant's family could offer assistance. Again, brands loved the concept.

11

Secrets and lies

*The most dangerous untruths are truths
moderately distorted*

Georg Christoph Lichtenberg, eighteenth-century German
satirist and scientist

During the 1950s, as America built confidence at home it generated distrust from overseas. Rogue states needed harnessing. To protect its political and commercial interests, the CIA set to work spinning out vote-winning stories, adorned with clichés and heroic statements designed to win the approval of the woefully ignorant American people.

―――――――

Soul traders advising politicians needed to show that they were looking after the interests of the electorate both at home and overseas. The Cold War offered the perfect political opportunity for a government to demonstrate its own brand of care for the national community. Such a stage was perfect for soul traders, enabling them to conduct a show of intrigue that was so enthralling it would put even the most riveting TV program to shame.

In 1953 the Soviet Union produced propaganda movies appealing for calm over nuclear threats. At the same time, both British and American governments warned that the threat of communism was everywhere.

In Iran, Prime Minister Mohammed Mosaddeq, who was increasingly succumbing to communist influence, declared Britain an enemy. Through the Anglo-Iranian Oil Company (AIOC), Britain had considerable vested interests in the country's oil reserves. Despite its international ties and support, the company was nationalized. Mosaddeq's empathy towards communism was enough for Britain to ask America to intervene.

On April 4, 1953, America became involved in overthrowing a government when CIA director Allen Dulles approved $1 million to be used "in any way that would bring about the fall of Mosaddeq." The CIA's Tehran office set to work distributing as much anti-Mosaddeq propaganda as possible. On a signal broadcast by the BBC, Operation Ajax was put into action with the aim of securing a coup d'état in which the democratically elected Mosaddeq would be replaced with a pro-West dictatorship, headed by a new prime minister (Fazlollah Zahedi) and the Shah of Iran. By 1954, the Anglo-Iranian Oil Company had become BP (British Petroleum).

Having acquired a taste for propaganda, America looked elsewhere for opportunities to practice propaganda techniques and so boost the feel-good experience for the American people. The United Fruit Company controlled a large plantation in Guatemala. The country was run by Colonel Jacobo Árbenz Guzmán, a gregarious man who promised his people that he would empower the poor by ridding the nation of its dependence on America. A law was passed to confiscate the uncultivated portions of large plantations. The United Fruit Company's land had over 85 percent of its holdings uncultivated. Árbenz offered the company $3 per acre, although the company valued the land at $75 per acre.

By chance the United Fruit Company was intimately connected with the American government. The American Secretary of State, John Foster Dulles and his brother, Allen, worked for the company's rail subsidiary. Allen just happened to be Director of the CIA. The Under Secretary of State, Walter Bedell Smith, also enjoyed close commercial ties with the company.

After the communists gained four seats in government in 1952, they began to gain more influence in Guatemalan politics. Increasingly nervous, United Fruit called on the CIA to help. On February 19, 1954, the CIA instigated Operation Washtub, a cunning plan to plant a fake Soviet arms cache to demonstrate Guatemalan ties to Moscow. The American propaganda machine went full steam ahead. Soul traders saw the chance for headlines about protecting the American people against the communist threat to democracy. The CIA turned to Bernays to create a fake news agency called the Middle American Information Bureau.

Press releases were duly dispatched warning of Guatemala's imminent plan to use their beachheads to threaten America.

The CIA recommended a terror-bombing campaign to belittle Árbenz and his troops. Further press releases prepared for the tissue- and hairspray-buying public back home reassured them that America was doing its bit as the world's champion of democracy.

Árbenz tried several times to buy weapons from Western Europe but could only procure barely serviceable German World War II weaponry from the Czechs. When the Czechoslovak weaponry arrived aboard the Swedish ship *Alfhem*, Bernays used the evidence as final proof of Guatemala's communist allegiances.

After the coup, Árbenz resigned his office. Following five successive juntas occupying the presidential palace, the Americans finally approved of a suitable replacement—Carlos Castillo Armas. Visiting the new president in 1955, Richard Nixon said that President Castillo Armas' objective "is to do more for the people in two years than the communists were able to do in ten years. This is the first instance in history where a communist government has been replaced by a free one." It transpired, though, that Armas was a dictator who instituted many arbitrary rules, including denying illiterates the right to vote.

Back in America, reviewing the propaganda tactics of his nation, Bernays came to the conclusion that the soul-trading interests of business and politics were indivisible, and that when dealing with the masses it was just too difficult to explain big issues on a purely rational basis. What was needed was what Bernays called the "engineering of consent." This, in turn, paved the way for "engineering" people's minds to make them covet goods and services they didn't actually need. Soul traders simply had to link products, services and ideas to the unconscious desires and darkest drives of consumers and electors.

12

The 28 ways

Two ideas are always needed: one to kill the other

Georges Braque, French Cubist painter

All students of propaganda are well versed in the 28 techniques required to persuade anyone of anything: they flatter, they cajole, they create paranoia, they generate distrust, they affirm half-truths, and provoke the public to believing what is needed to be believed in order to build trust. Some techniques are as old as civilization itself. Modern states and totalitarian regimes still use many of these techniques. They are used, knowingly or unknowingly, by religious institutions, commercial spin-doctors, and politically correct bureaucracies and brands.

In this part of our journey, take a notebook and jot down the hidden persuader's unpublicized 101 rules as repeated throughout history and yet never openly acknowledged in campaigns. Then open your eyes to today's headlines and crusades and see things in a completely different light.

With two world wars under the belt and twentieth-century marketing and public relations entering its midlife years, corporate and commercial propaganda was no longer simply a series of haphazard techniques. It had emerged as a well-oiled machine, equipped with an arsenal of weapons and tools so well stocked that governments and corporations would use it for many years to come.

Ad hominem

Smear your adversary's character rather than addressing their argument.

A–B choice

Offer only two choices, with your cause or brand being the better of the two. You are either for us or against us. You're either a "brand-x" user or a nobody.

Repetition

Repeat your message time and time and time again via controlled use of the media. For example, use a political motto or an advertising jingle.

Arouse anxieties

Arouse paranoia about situations outside a well-established routine. For example, panic a society about an impending subversive overthrow by terrorists. Or market private health insurance to families concerned about the capabilities of a state-run national health service.

Highlight self-interests

Incorporate emotive terms highlighting ethical fairness, or point to the selfishness of a second party's interests over that of the greater good. For example, "any honest person wouldn't dream of paying for a counterfeit brand," or "Bureaucrats always put up barriers to prevent change."

Get them onboard

Encourage people to feel accepted, rather than ostracized. Get them to join a group of peers committed to a cause that promises the real prospect of success.

Expert blessing

Secure and exploit the voluntary or sponsored endorsement of a respected expert, politician or celebrity. Expert testimonials seal a proposition. In deference, the target audience capitulates to the proposition put forward by authorities or brands, believing that "if it is good enough for the experts who independently understand the implications of the cause, it must be good enough for everyone."

Hold on tight

Reassure those steadfast to your brand or cause that loyalty, however difficult it is to stick to, is the best moral as well as the most logical course of action. Indeed, the act of having to endure awkward or testing rules will build personal character and gain longer-term reward. This technique is often used in religions or cults.

Be one of the in-crowd

Make people believe their loyalty proves that they are trendsetters rather than followers. In marketing, this works well with brands appealing to youth, such as Reebok sneakers or Apple iPods. Another example that comes to mind is an advert published by Burger King against McDonald's, reading, "Would you rather feast like a king or eat like a clown?"

Big lie

Continually repeat your version of a set of events that have led to a current situation until the audience begins to believe your account. Continue to do so even if on close examination your story can't be fully substantiated. The only steadfast rule to follow is that your story must contain a grain of truth that's just enough to make your account plausible.

One of the people

Present your campaign in terms and language understood by the average person in the street. This technique, referred to as "plain folks" by the Institute for Propaganda Analysis, shows you are accessible, witty and one of the people rather than the distant elite. Advertisers often use this technique to incorporate a sense of humility and even humor in their products or services. For example, Virgin Atlantic ran a series of posters promoting their extra-wide seats and in-flight entertainment using the headlines, "9 inches of pleasure" and "Play with yourself." In 1949, hoping to appeal to teenagers, Brylcreem published the slogan, "A little dab'll do ya."

Demonize the enemy

Position the enemy as being at worst subhuman and at best sinister. For example, Hitler demonized Jews before and during World War II. America demonized Vietnam War combatants as "gooks" during the Vietnam War. In 2007, demonizing Israel and America, Iranian President Mahmoud Ahmadinejad said: "People of the world, put your trust in God . . . The era of darkness will end, prisoners will return home, the occupied lands will be freed, Palestine and Iraq will be liberated from the domination of the occupiers, and the people of America and Europe will be free of the pressures exerted by the Zionists. The tender-hearted and humanity-loving governments will replace the aggressive and domineering ones. Human dignity will be regained."

Direct order

Sometimes the best way to get a complicated message across is to keep it simple and authoritative. For example: Nike's advertising slogan "Just do it"; the Mars slogan "A Mars a day helps you work, rest and play"; the World War I Lord Kitchener poster stating, "Your country needs you."

Euphoria

Concentrate on a central event around which a campaign is built. By doing so a soul trader draws the target audience's attention away from other issues that may demotivate them.

In the early build-up to the London 2012 Olympic games, the British government published stories of how the Games would help turn around the economy as well as the state of the nation's health. In August 2008 an investigation by the *Independent on Sunday* uncovered an estimated £1.3 million lobbying endeavor by companies competing for a share in the £9.3 billion Olympics budget for the 2012 Games. The "freebies" included VIP tickets to the opera as well as England soccer, rugby and cricket matches, champagne receptions, garden parties and extravagant lunches and dinners.

Disinformation

An old adage goes, "Seeing is believing." The proliferation of popular photography during the twentieth century helped propagandists promote causes through carefully doctored or misinterpreted visual evidence. The Nazis used photographs of mentally ill patients to justify a program of euthanasia.

In 1954, to prove Guatemala's collaboration with the USSR, Richard Nixon showed the press pictures of piles of Marxist literature allegedly found in the President's palace. In the lead-up to the bombing of Iraq by the Western Coalition of countries led by America and Britain, photographic evidence of a large shed in Iraq was shown to the press, with claims that it was a likely venue for storing weapons of mass destruction.

During the 2006 conflict between Israel and Lebanon, Adnan Haji, a Reuters photographer, published a doctored photograph purporting to show bomb damage to the city of Beirut. On closer examination, the plumes of smoke in the picture were revealed as fakes added to the scene using Photoshop manipulation software. Movies showing dead Palestinians allegedly killed by Israeli firepower were proved to have been staged for the world's media. This came to light when a covert cameraman filmed the "dead bodies" miraculously climbing to their feet once the Palestinian PR people believed the world's news camera crews had left the scene.

In July 2008 Iran released photographs of missiles being tested. The pictures appeared on the front pages of the *Los Angeles Times*, the *Financial Times*, the *Chicago Tribune* and several other newspapers as well as being broadcast on BBC News, MSNBC, and major news websites. But the pictures were not quite what they at first seemed. They originated via Agence France-Presse, which claimed it obtained the images from the website of Sepah News, the media arm of the Iranian Revolutionary Guards. Four missiles appeared to be on the brink of being launched. However, after the agency distributed the picture, Associated Press circulated what appeared to be a nearly identical photo from the same source, but without the fourth missile. In order to make the arsenal appear more sinister, the extra missile was added using Photoshop. Agence France-Presse retracted its four-missile photograph, saying that the image was "apparently digitally altered" by Iranian state media. (Also see "Pleading for justice in the court of world opinion" on page 206.)

Sometimes soul traders sway the media towards a single, desired line simply by addressing human laziness. Public relations professionals occasionally distribute "Video News Releases" (VNRs) to the press. These are pre-filmed announcements regarding product launches or new ventures. In addition to being produced to broadcast quality, VNRs include hardcopy supplementary journalist scripts. If a local TV company is up against a deadline they may use the footage and even read the script, claiming to have filmed and researched the entire piece themselves, and so betraying journalistic impartiality.

Glittering generalizations

When people can't quite put their finger on why a product, service or cause is worth pursuing, soul traders may opt for glittering generalizations. For example: "Makers of the world's finest products" (Philip Morris); "Striving to make the world a better place" (Ford Motor Company); "You've got a friend in the business" (Gateway Computers); "Putting customers first . . . ," "Putting quality first . . ." (both used by countless "me-too" brands).

Opponents of America's invasion and occupation of Iraq used the slogan "blood for oil," suggesting that the invasion was carried out solely to gain access to Iraq's oil. Hawks arguing that America should continue its campaign in Iraq adopted the slogan "cut and run," thereby suggesting that it would be cowardly to withdraw.

In wartime soul traders in public relations encourage the media to adopt national war slogans as banners in captions carrying a message of unity to readers and viewers. Such slogans have included "enduring freedom," "war on terror," and "just cause."

In 2007 Hilary Benn, the British Secretary of State responsible for International Development, claimed that rather than acting as a motto of defiance against a common enemy, the American phrase "war on terror" actual strengthened extremist groups. For this reason the British government dropped the slogan.

Worthy words

Nothing reassures people quite like positive encouragement. Worthy words are apt, positive reaffirmations, and when freely sprinkled within a propaganda statement they create an upbeat image that can be associated with a cause. For example: "Peace," "happiness," "family," "wise leadership," "freedom," "truth," and so on.

Half-truth

John Wannamaker (1838–1922) is credited for first having said, "Half of my advertising works, I just don't know which half." This statement sounds reasonable and even perceptive. Yet it camouflages a deeper deceit. In fact for most organizations, not even half their advertising works. For example, these days in direct mail, most brands would be lucky if even one percent of their advertising worked.

Andy Tarshis of A. C. Nielsen once said, "We found advertising works the way the grass grows. You can never see it, but every week you have to mow the lawn." I recall in my youth listening to direct-mail marketing gurus like Drayton Bird evangelize that direct marketing was far better than general advertising because whereas in general adverting half the budget was unquantifiable, direct marketers guaranteed to deliver around a three percent response.

Entire direct marketing agencies and even advertising empires were built on selling that "three percent guarantee," somehow luring marketers into a false sense of security and ignoring the fact that 97 percent of their spend would be wasted! Half-truths are powerful tools ideal for open interpretation. For example, in the 1990s a survey of 10,000 British households conducted by Taylor Nelson Sofres discovered that shoppers who bought their groceries from Tesco were keen on special offers and enjoyed fish. Sainsbury's shoppers also liked fish, as did Waitrose shoppers. But Iceland and Somerfield shoppers considered themselves as "homely." Perhaps . . . but really, who cares?

Reductio ad Hitlerum

This technique states that if an evil or undesirable faction supports, uses or performs something in particular, then that object or concept must be horrific. So if hoodlums carry penknives, all penknives are automatically reclassified as weapons rather than tools. In public relations this can be useful, as culpability gets shifted from the villain to the object or set of beliefs (in this case, knives). This creates the opportunity for lots of political spin in news stories about knives, which of course in the long term are irrelevant, as the real problem isn't knives but the way they are misused.

Oversimplification

Soul traders love to portray products or services as simplifiers of life's often tedious, everyday tasks. This popular advertising strategy was often deployed in the 1950s to sell "white" and "brown goods" (kitchen equipment such as fridges and furniture). It remains a popular technique to sell anything from washing whiteners to kitchen cleaners: "Bang! And the dirt is gone" (Cillit Bang!).

Contextomy

Documentary makers occasionally edit programs to paint people's actions or words in a completely different light than the subject intended. In the hands of politicians, this technique can be a highly effective way of manipulating public opinion. Even popular sayings which most believe are accurate may not always be so. For example, Sigmund Freud is quoted as having said, "Dreams are the royal road to consciousness." In fact this is only a summary of the full quote, which is: "The interpretation of dreams is the royal road to knowledge of the unconscious activities of the mind." Sherlock Holmes's catchphrase "Elementary, my dear Watson" was never written by Conan Doyle but came from a movie review in the *New York Times*, October 19, 1929. The line "Play it again, Sam" is famously attributed to Humphrey Bogart in the movie *Casablanca*, but Bogart actually said, "If she can stand it, I can. Play it!" His supporting lead, Ingrid Bergman, replied, "Play it, Sam. Play 'As Time Goes By'."

More controversial examples of this editing can be found in translations of Arabic to English. In August 2001, the American TV channel CBS aired an interview with a Hamas activist, Muhammad Abu Wardeh, who recruited terrorists for suicide bombings in Israel. Wardeh was quoted as saying: "God would compensate the martyr for sacrificing his life for his land. If you become a martyr, God will give you 70 virgins, 70 wives and everlasting happiness." Yet since September 11, 2001, some (not all) Muslim scholars have repeatedly explained that suicide is forbidden in Islam. Suicide (*qatlu nafsi-hi*) is forbidden in the

Traditions (Hadith in Arabic), which are the collected sayings and doings attributed to the Prophet Muhammad and traced back to him through a series of putatively trustworthy witnesses.

As for the rewards in paradise, the Quran describes Islamic paradise in exquisite detail. For instance, Quran sura 56 verses 12–38 (Penguin translation by N. J. Dawood) says:

> "They shall recline on jewelled couches face to face, and there shall wait on them immortal youths with bowls and ewers and a cup of purest wine (that will neither pain their heads nor take away their reason); with fruits of their own choice and flesh of fowls that they relish. And theirs shall be the dark-eyed houris, chaste as hidden pearls: a guerdon for their deeds . . . We created the houris and made them virgins, loving companions for those on the right hand . . ."

Many translations explain the Arabic (plural) word *Abkarun* as "virgins"; however, some Muslims claim there has been a mistranslation, that "virgins" should be replaced by "angels." In sura 55 verses 72–74, Dawood translates the Arabic word "hur" or "hūrīya" as "virgins," but interestingly the Quran never mentions a definite number of virgins in paradise. Also the houris are available for all Muslims, not exclusively martyrs.

In 1988 Salman Rushdie wrote one of the twentieth century's most notorious books, *The Satanic Verses*. In the novel Rushdie struck at the very tenets of Islam and it was seen by some fanatical Muslims to be blasphemous. On the other hand, many literary scholars interpreted the work as a brilliant tale relating to Rushdie's personal identity crisis. According to interpretation and context Rushdie's work can be represented in various ways, dependent upon the observer's political or religious motives.

Rationalization

Experienced marketers are acquainted with the notion of cognitive dissonance (see page 66). Once a choice of brand is made, even if that brand turns out to be more expensive than the competition, providing the consumer has invested enough of his or her personal time and energy into planning the purchase, the person will be convinced that their decision was wise.

Red herring

The first technique to be mastered by magicians is sleight of hand. Distract an audience and the rest is easy. Spin doctors are well aware of the technique. In the lead-up to the 2003 invasion of Iraq, the Coalition said that there was evidence to suggest that Saddam Hussein had the capability to launch weapons of mass destruction that could reach Britain within 45 minutes, and this was an important argument in justifying the invasion. Despite all the subsequent reports and research, no hard evidence was ever proven. (See "Disinformation," page 104.)

Similar to the Red Herring technique is "card stacking." Audience perception of an issue is manipulated by emphasizing one thing whilst ignoring or repressing another. For example, creating media events focusing on a particular view, using one-sided testimonials, or making sure that any voices of dissent are either ridiculed or silenced.

Euphemism

Political correctness (PC) in advertising turns a diet concoction of water, carbon dioxide, orange, lemon, lime, ginseng, ginkgo bilboa, l-carnitine, sugar, vitamin C, caffeine, taurine, guarana and vitamin B for fat people into a "health drink" for "cuddly" people. In health care, wrinkle cream becomes "rejuvenating moisturiser." In marketing meetings, brainstorms become "thought showers." In politics, euphemisms turn death by bombs and bullets into "collateral damage." Even the dead become the "metabolically disabled."

But sometimes things slip through the PC censors' net. In 2008, Intel, the computer chip maker, apologized for an advertisement showing six black sprinters crouched in the starting position in front of a white man in an office wearing a shirt and chinos. The headline read: "Multiply computer performance and maximize the power of your employees." Don MacDonald, director of global marketing for the company Intel, wrote in a corporate blog: "We made a bad mistake. I know why and how, but that simply doesn't make it better."

During the Reagan Administration the MX-missile was renamed "the Peacekeeper." In the 1940s America changed the name of its War Department to the "Department of Defense." During World War I, soldiers who became mentally disturbed by the physical and psychological impact of the battleground were said to be "shell-shocked"—a sweetened euphemism giving the impression that they were simply "in shock" from having heard quite loud bangs. Many generals considered the condition a sign of cowardice. Victims were treated with electric shocks; some underwent psychotherapeutic treatment to restore normality.

Decades later, having learned the error of their ways, the military renamed the condition "combat fatigue," but that term simply painted a quaint picture of soldiers feeling rather tired after a hard day at the front. Following the Vietnam War, the condition was renamed again, this time as "post-traumatic stress disorder."

During the Iraq War of 2003, the military came up with a reverse euphemism for shell shock relating to the "shock" experienced by civilians rather than army personnel. "Shock and awe" suggested the reverence that the Iraqi people were meant to have for the Coalition forces' firepower. The term is an allusion to the Old Testament:

"All the people witnessed the thunder and lightning, the blare of the horn and the mountain smoking; and when the people saw it, they fell back and stood at a distance. 'You speak to us,' they said to Moses, 'and we will obey: but let not God speak to us, lest we die.' Moses answered the people, 'Be not afraid; for God has come only in order to test you and in order that the fear of Him may be with ever with you, so that you do not go astray'.
Exodus 20:15–18

Dysphemism

This is used to harm the reputation of or lessen the perceived quality of a group, ideology or entity. A soul trader might use dysphemism to discredit a body without defaming it. For example, "liberal" is a dysphemism which could be positioned to suggest a group without any steadfast ideals. During the Cold War, the word "Soviets" was turned into a dysphemism suggesting a sinister force for evil. In the USSR, the term "the United States" became a dysphemism for a belligerent nation of selfish capitalists.

Whipping boy

It was him, not me! Assigning blame to an individual or group alleviates feelings of guilt in the parties actually responsible. It offers soul traders the chance to distract attention away from dealing with the real cause of a problem.

Stereotyping, name calling and labeling

Labeling a group as something to be feared, hated, loathed, or rejected is a technique that attempts to arouse prejudices. For instance, in 2007 Republican Governor Romney said:

"The new generation of challenges we face includes challenges to our national security as well. These violent

Jihadists are intent on replacing moderate Muslim governments with a caliphate or an Imam. And they seek of course the collapse of our economy and our government and our military."

In an article in 1937 entitled "How The Jews Can Combat Persecution," Winston Churchill wrote:

"The central fact which dominates the relations of Jew and non-Jew is that the Jew is 'different'. He looks different. He thinks differently. He has a different tradition and background. He refuses to be absorbed."

Cambridge University historian Richard Toye discovered the article in the university's archive of Churchill's papers. Toye claimed that Churchill's secretary advised that it would be "inadvisable" to publish the article and at the time it never saw the light of day.

Notwithstanding these comments, elsewhere in the article Churchill praised Jews as "sober, industrious, law-abiding," and urged Britons to stand up for the race against persecution.

Transferable association

The subject of semiotics is concerned with understanding signs and symbols. Semiotics breaks down the components of signs into signifiers (the form that the sign takes) and the signified (the concept it represents). The sign is the whole that results from the association of the signifier with the signified. The relationship between the signifier and the signified is known as signification.

The swastika, which came to signify Nazi dominance, originally had a different meaning. The goddess Artemis is said to have had a female triangle with a swastika symbol drawn on her stomach. The same emblem, called the "Cross of Thor," can also be found on ancient coins. In Hinduism the swastika represents health and prosperity and the revered Lord Ganesh wore the swastika on his right hand. Julius Caesar was the first to brand the pursuit of power and pleasure under the emblem of an eagle. The Nazis and Americans later both adopted the eagle.

Transferable association comes into play when an image associated with one school of thought is superimposed over another. For example, in America, anti-war protestors may superimpose the garments of Osama Bin Laden on the body of the American president. When designed as satirical sketches, cartoons often offer witty comments on political characters and situations. However, cartoons have also long been used as manipulative weapons of propaganda to reach an audience who normally wouldn't read in-depth articles, or to be passed on to wider audiences. Over the years, propaganda cartoons have been used to support political agendas, cunningly providing vicious attacks on people of different cultures, from Jews and Muslims to many other cultural and ethnic groups.

Some Arab-language newspapers, such as the Kuwaiti *Al-Watan* and *Al-Quds* and others, regularly publish anti-Semitic cartoons with themes such as demonization of Jews and zoomorphism (showing Jews as animals or insects), comparing the Jewish State of Israel with the Third Reich and perpetuating the myth of the blood libel (a Greek anti-Semitic myth that was resurrected in twelfth-century England, when it was alleged that Jews in Norwich had killed a young boy in order to use his Christian blood for their Passover service). In January 2003, on Holocaust Remembrance Day, cartoonist Dave Brown published a cartoon in the British newspaper the *Independent* showing the Israeli Prime Minister Ariel Sharon eating Palestinian babies. In 2006, newspapers reprinted a cartoon showing the holy prophet Muhammad with a suicide bomb as a turban.

The difference between a top-flight creative man and the hack is his ability to express powerful meanings indirectly

Vance Packard

The manipulative 28 tools of propaganda would have had a familiar ring to a certain American journalist, Vance Packard, who understood the game of authoritative exploitation. In 1957, Packard published a groundbreaking book, *The Hidden Persuaders*, in which he brought to the public's attention the manipulative practices of big brands looking to win the souls rather than just the minds of the public. Packard yearned for the days when respected brands dealt with simple features and focused on the practical benefits of products, rather than making spurious and over-complicated emotional pitches. It was Packard who first implied that advertising was full of subliminal messages.

At this time, advertising agencies paid psychoanalysts to run focus groups (called "panel reaction" and "group interviews.") Through free-association techniques consumers were encouraged to openly discuss their feelings about products and services. Reported attitudes were then neatly compartmentalized into "product," "features," and "empathy." It was deduced that housewives wanted more than just convenience; they demanded to reclaim their skills as individuals. So products started to be marketed as statements of individualism: cake-mix manufacturers began to include instructions to add an egg to mixtures, not because the ingredients were incomplete without the egg but because the act of cracking an egg made the housewife feel that she had made an essential personalized contribution to the entire baking process.

From this point on soul traders sold products, services, commodities, even celebrities and politicians based not just on what each could actually do but on how they connected emotionally with consumers, businesses and voters. Presidents would be elected on personality traits, family bonds, their looks and their attitude to extramarital relationships, as well as on the more traditional basis of manifestos and track records.

Packard intended his work to bring the deviant practices of marketing to the consciousness of the general public and help them to make more informed choices. He pointed out how industry creates a yearning for new brands by introducing ever-increasing lines of planned obsolescence. In the long run, however, the book had the opposite effect. Advertising and marketing proliferated; it filled every space—from radio commercials in the morning, to spam over the internet and streets plastered with billboards. People weren't blind to the neon signs and TV commercials, but they also thought that they weren't dumb, that clever advertising would "sucker" everyone else not them—they thought they were too sophisticated to be taken in.

Even when consumers were fully aware of being pampered and manipulated, they openly welcomed the indulgence. After all, millions of dollars of marketing budgets had been invested in making them feel like a king or a queen, not just for a day but for as long as they wanted the moment to last. Yet thanks to constantly improved new products, those moments soon turned out to be nothing more than a consumerist treadmill.

13

From the Cold War to mind bending

Holy molars! Am I ever glad I take good care of my teeth!

1960s *Batman* series

The 1960s saw a new kind of soul trader who took up the challenge from Vance Packard to spin out fantastic interpretations of everything from the Cold War to burgers and consumer psychology.

Enter the age of value-added lifestyles. The sixties set out to define what it was to be an individual. Psychologists, sportswear producers, hippies, ad men, Bozo the Clown and nuns led the shift in society. Soul traders manipulated masses searching for purpose in their lives. That meaning was delivered by encouraging them to buy products and services.

By the mid-1960s, society was beginning to tire of rock 'n' roll's incessant thud. A more laid-back melody with an assertive baseline was needed. Even Freud's ideas suggesting that most people needed to control their repressed urges were slowly losing favor. Soul traders recognized that society wanted to shake free.

Rather than passively conforming, people aggressively questioned all authority: adults, advertisers, politicians, and police. From New York to London, students protested against government and corporations. Activists claimed that rather than serve the people, the real agenda of big business was to draw attention away from the political calamities being conducted in their names—such as in Vietnam.

The philosopher Herbert Marcuse spoke regularly at student rallies. In his book *One-Dimensional Man*, published in 1964, Marcuse argued that mass-produced products diminished people's ability to express their feelings. He claimed that such bloated consumerism achieved little more than creating a simple way to market goods to "One-Dimensional Man." The students dug his rhetoric. Before long he was adopted as the father of the new left.

In 1967 Bob Dylan released his album *Subterranean Homesick Blues*, which inspired young Americans to form radically left groups such as the Weather Underground Organization, aka the Weathermen, to organize mass riots and even bombings in order to show their resentment of media-controlled society, materialism and the Vietnam War. Speaking to reporters during the Vietnam conflict, one of the founders of the Weathermen, Bernardine Dohrn, said, "There's no way to be committed to non-violence in the middle of the most violent society that history's ever created." The American government was having none of it. They fought back with tear gas and rubber bullets. On January 6, 1967, *Time* magazine wrote:

"In 1966, the young American became vociferously sceptical of the Great Society. Though he retains a strong emotional identification with the deprived and spurned citizens of his own and other societies, he recognizes that the civil rights revolution, in which he was an early hero at the barricades, has reached a stage at which his own involvement is no longer vital. And, as a letter to the President signed by 100 student leaders across the nation showed last week, he has become increasing perturbed by the war. [Youthful Americans protested the rigidity and elitism of their universities, and through their actions they expressed the frustration, rage and alienation felt by many of the young about racial inequality, social injustice, the Vietnam War and the economic and political constraints of conventional life and work.]"

While the student riots were tempestuous, the overwhelming firepower of the state police meant they couldn't be sustained indefinitely. Even the marketing professionals in Madison Avenue, New York (by then synonymous with the glitzy world of advertising and public relations), recognized that it was time to cut through the corpulence of corporate promises and instead deliver a lean and mean message that hit the spot. Agencies like Papert, Koenig, Lois Inc. produced stark advertisements for clients such as the Committee for a Sane Nuclear Policy with the headline "1.25 million unborn children will be born dead or have some gross defect because of Nuclear Bomb testing."

It wasn't me who won gold—but it will be
Nike advertisement to commemorate the countdown to the 2012 London Olympic Games

The Cold War offered soul traders unforeseen opportunities. Non-Western countries competed for the title of "country most oppressed by capitalist imperialism." Writer and intellectual Lu Xun Lu Xun (or Lu Hsün) wrote: "Throughout the ages, the Chinese have had only one way of looking at foreigners. We either look up to them or down on them as wild animals." In the Cold War mentality of the 1960 Olympic Games, the Eastern Bloc allies claimed that every medal won was further evidence of the superiority of their political systems.

One racist West German sprinter, Armin Hary, saw the Games as a financial opportunity. He refused to meet with Jesse Owens, an African-American sprinter who in the 1936 Nazi-managed Berlin Games had won four gold medals. Owens was in Rome as a journalist writing a syndicated column for a Chicago newspaper. Hary ended up winning the 100-meter sprint, defeating the American sprinter Dave Sime in a photo finish. Hary was the first non-American to win the race since 1928.

German marketers seized on Hary's national victory, persuading him to accept "under the table" payments for wearing branded running shoes. In return Hary wore two brands. One was Adidas, named after its founder, Adolf (Adi) Dassler, and the other was Puma, founded in 1948 by his brother Rudolf. Puma was set up in direct competition with Adidas. Hary wore the Adidas shoes in the race then hid them in his kit bag, from which he pulled out a pair of Puma shoes to wear when accepting his gold medal. The 1960 Olympics were also notable as the first televised Games, which meant that they attracted even more commercial branding. CBS paid under half a million dollars for the broadcast rights and sent just under 50 people to cover the event. In contrast, by 2008 NBC was paying $1 billion for the right to cover the Beijing Olympics, and sent 2,900 people to produce some 1,400 hours of TV coverage and a further 2,200 hours of coverage on the Web. Today soul traders openly brand athletes: the 2008 American Olympic basketball squad was virtually totally financed by Nike.

What we need is a great big melting pot.
Big enough to take the world and all it's got.
Keep it stirring for a hundred years or more.
Turning out coffee-colored people by the score.
Blue Mink, "Melting Pot"

In 1968, free expression wasn't just on the track and TV. Eight years after the last 1960 Olympic athlete broke through the finishing line, women's liberation jerked its last juddering days before reaching its full climax. Erica Jong completed final drafts of her book *Fear of Flying*. Philip Morris, the people behind the all-testosterone Marlboro brand, introduced Virginia Slims, a cigarette aimed at the newly emancipated self-reliant woman, with the slogan "You've come a long way, baby," devised by advertising agency Leo Burnett. The hippy movement urged people to put down their weapons of mass discontent and instead find serenity by making peace with their inner selves, an exercise invariably aided with a good long drag of "a cool smoke."

Setting up headquarters in California, the Esalen Institute was established by a group of psychoanalysts to provide a place where people could exorcise inner negative feelings that society had previously deemed should be repressed. The center's reputation as a means to feel enlightened and liberated grew so much that, by the early seventies, Esalen was a national cause rather than a local *cause célèbre*. It gave rise to the Human Potential Movement, which drew much of its inspiration from Abraham Maslow's theory of the hierarchy of needs. Soul traders would usurp this later as a major tenet of marketing. Esalen believed that all people, regardless of creed or color, could realize their potential by working in groups. This philosophy had a huge influence not just in the West but also in the Middle East. Israel saw the rapid reemergence of the utopian Kibbutz movement. Kibbutzim were socialist-based collective enterprises, but operated within a free-market system.

Nevertheless, the Alexandre Dumas ideology of "all for one and one for all" didn't go down well with everyone. Black radical groups suspected that hippy-based movements were in reality little more than white liberals seeking to undermine the collective identity and power of blacks. Having endured decades of racial abuse, the last thing blacks wanted was to be forced to integrate into a world where rules and regulations were dictated by whites, albeit well-intentioned ones. Clearly love and mutual respect between brothers and sisters of humanity wasn't going to be something that could be fixed with a couple of open-minded hippy sessions. However, while love of all mankind might not be easy to bring about, love between man and woman, woman and woman and man and man was something else.

A group of radical psychotherapists approached one of America's largest religious seminaries, the Convent of the Immaculate Heart. They wanted to see if nuns could find greater happiness in openly expressing their dormant feelings than from "the good book." Encounter workshops were held for hundreds of nuns at a time. Having been reintroduced to fundamental emotions that had been repressed by the Church, the nuns came to the conclusion that their true needs were in direct conflict with imposed beliefs and virtues.

They demanded respect as the women they really were, rather than be forced to hide in habits that concealed their deeper human spirit. The nuns wanted the latest fashions and more. One nun, having discovered her latent lesbianism, even seduced another. Within a year half the convent petitioned the Vatican to be released from their vows; all that remained was a small group of radicalized lesbian nuns. The convent was forced to close its gates for good.

The story of the Convent of the Immaculate Heart might sound like a piece of utterly insignificant sensationalism, or perhaps the basis for an early 1970s porn-movie plot, but in reality it reflected a radical shift in society. People wanted to make the most of now. In America, conscription into the services in the 1960s meant that the young had to make the most of their lives while they could. Traditional products and services like life insurance saw a tumble in sales. Who wanted to plan for tomorrow when you should live for the moment? Consumers demanded products that enhanced self-expression.

Business was geared up to producing a limited variety of mass-market goods. Until then, society had only requested what corporations told it it wanted. Such a business model was easy to execute. But now consumers were becoming awkward. They suddenly demanded brands in infinite variations reflecting their personal tastes and desires. Just as young women personalized their miniskirts and blouses with trinkets, so brands would now have to deliver according to the consumers' whim. Not only that, but goods had to be bigger and better. It was all entirely in keeping with the sentiments of Frank Sinatra's 1969 hit song "My Way."

"Hey Mac, do you want fries with that brand— you Bozo?"

One brand with national outlets recognizing the need to give local consumers more of what they wanted was McDonald's. In 1967 the company reinvented the traditional burger, turning it from a patty between two bun halves into the Big Mac. The company had grown tremendously since 1937, when two brothers, Dick and Mac McDonald, opened a hot dog stand in Arcadia, California. By 1953, the company had grown through franchises and by 1955, under the strong business guidance of Ray Kroc, it began to be run as a major organization. By 1958, McDonald's had sold its 100 millionth burger.

In 1961, on little more than a handshake, the McDonald brothers sold Kroc their rights for $2.7 million, which was also meant to include an overriding royalty of 1 percent on the gross sales. As this clause wasn't in writing, Kroc ignored the royalty portion of the agreement. The brothers kept their original restaurant, but failed to retain rights to remain a McDonald's franchise. The brothers renamed their remaining restaurant "The Big M." However, Kroc forced them out of business, opening a McDonald's just one block away. Had the original deal between Kroc and the brothers been upheld, the brother's descendants would have earned around $100 million per year.

In 1963, Kroc recognized the potential in targeting children and families. He encouraged a Washington DC franchisee to sponsor a WRC-TV program called *Bozo the Clown*. William Scott, who played the clown, was employed to play the role of Ronald Mac. Scott was later interviewed by the Food Network program. Recalling the early days he said:

> "At the time, Bozo was the hottest children's show on the air. You could probably have sent Pluto the dog or Dumbo the elephant over and it would have been equally as successful.

But I was there, and I was Bozo . . . There was something about the combination of hamburgers and Bozo that was irresistible to kids . . . That's why when Bozo went off the air a few years later, the local McDonald's people asked me to come up with a new character to take Bozo's place. So, I sat down and created Ronald McDonald."

According to the website thinkquest.org, Ronald McDonald became the second-best-known person in the world. Only Santa Claus was better known.

Millions of mind guerrillas . . . Raising the spirit of peace and love, not war

John Lennon, "Mind Games"

While McDonald's was serving Big Macs, Madison Avenue was chewing over how to make their clients' products and services more appealing to the new generation of non-conformist consumers. Talking to a non-conformist was a non-starter. None of them wanted to attend formal conformist focus groups! So the ad men, often dressed in neatly pressed suits, had to second-guess what the people wearing Afghan coats really wanted. Many had heard of the techniques used by the Human Potential Movement and so started to peel product propositions down to their core. However, just as the ad men were about to reach the final layer of identity, one man, Werner Erhard, introduced the masses to EST (Erhard Seminar Training).

Rather than reduce people to their center, EST peeled away even further, revealing nothing: no meaning, no belief. Zero. Only from nothing, argued Erhard, could a person finally become someone—an individual answerable only to themselves rather than to brands, politicians or even God.

14

Maslow, microchips and the pursuit of happiness

Propaganda, to be effective, must be believed. To be believed, it must be credible. To be credible, it must be true.

Hubert H. Humphrey, American Vice President, 1965–1969

Get out your bell-bottom jeans, pull on your Nikes, grab a Coke and open your Windows. The 1970s saw the beginnings of movements that set out to shrink the world and change ideas of class distinction to such an extent that even the nerdiest of geeks or the most resolutely middle-class families would feel they could reach their full potential.

Advertisers, technologists and spin doctors became obsessed with putting people and information into neat little boxes. Two men in particular were responsible for this. One explained human motives while the other introduced the world to the power of microchips. The means to become better informed about what really constitutes happiness and self-awareness changed radically and virtually overnight.

The new landscape we find ourselves in has changed the roadmap for marketing communications forever.

The arrival of the 1970s was a time for the soul traders to step in and reintroduce substance to consumers. The Stanford Research Institute (SRI) offered businesses a way to understand how to make sure that products, services and even commodities could appear tailor-made for the individual even when such items were in fact mass-produced.

A consumer measurement system called Value Added Lifestyles (VALS) was formulated. It explained the whims and wishes of consumers. VALS segmented groups into types based on the same model that inspired the Human Potential Movement (from Abraham Maslow's hierarchy of needs). For the first time ordinary people were invited to complete questionnaires to reveal what really motivated them. This enabled researchers to fit consumers into Maslow's categories. SRI discovered that there was a huge group of people who refused to be defined by either society, marketing or political soul traders. This group believed that they defined themselves; these were the so-called "inner directives." For them, personal satisfaction was more important than status or money. They were self-expressive, complex and individualistic.

Another group, the "I-am-me's," were very much of the early 1980s punk era: they broke away from traditions in order to invent their own fashions and outlooks. "Experientials" were happy to have a go at anything—at least once—from new sports to new trends. Yet another group, the "societally conscious," were concerned with issues such as the environment, world politics and conservation.

All your life they will tell you "no," quite firmly and very quickly. And you will tell them "yes."
Nike advertisement

In 1971, the same year that a computer nerd called Ray Tomlinson sent himself the world's first email, a young "societally conscious" graphic design student, Carolyn Davidson from Portland State University, befriended a temporary accountancy teacher called Phil Knight. Phil ran a sportswear company called Blue Ribbon Sports.

Recognizing Carolyn's graphic design skills he asked her to draw promotional concepts for a new line of athletic footwear. At the rate of $2 an hour, Carolyn drew a tick mark—the "swoosh"— and presented a bill for $35. By 1972 the Nike "swoosh" was seen on the trainers of American track and field Olympic trial athletes in Oregon. Within decades that "swoosh" would be seen in just about every corner of world, and yes, happily, Carolyn was later more fully compensated for her designs.

While Carolyn doodled, 12,000 anti-war militants attempted to disrupt government business in Washington. Australia and New Zealand eventually withdrew their troops from Vietnam, and by December 1971 the American administration reduced troop numbers serving in Vietnam to their lowest-ever figures. Also in the same year, Coca-Cola released a commercial showing young men and women of every color and race clutching bottles of Coca-Cola. In harmony and with great emotion they sang:

"I'd like to build the world a home and furnish it with love. Grow apple trees and honeybees and snow-white turtledoves. I'd like to teach the world to sing (sing with me), in perfect harmony. I'd like to buy the world a Coke and keep it company (that's the real thing). I'd like to teach the world to sing in perfect harmony. I'd like to buy the world a Coke and keep it company. It's the real thing— Coke is. What the world wants today—Coca-Cola. It's the real thing."

The commercial became more than a homage to Pemberton's original French Wine Cola. By now the brand was god, peace, love and happiness—all contained in a pregnant-shaped glass bottle (the bottle inspired by C. S. Root's original design of a coca bean). Coca-Cola was ready to deliver a new generation of hope in the face of gloom. The soul traders had given the "societally conscious" the means to teach world leaders a lesson in how to sing in harmony rather than scream in anger.

Remaining true to Maslow's basic hierarchy of needs, SRI went on to produce more neatly defined consumer categories. All were designed to help big business as well as politicians offer consumers and voters not just products or ideals, but icons providing a sense of belonging to groups with purpose. Audiences asserted allegiance to brands and in doing so became persuaded to buy or vote for almost anything. This was not just because of the obvious benefits; it was also because of the promise of being able to belong to a group.

Who was Maslow?

Abraham Maslow was a brilliant professor of psychology at Brandeis University, Boston. The son of pushy Soviet immigrants, he spent his early life taking refuge in books. Receiving a BA in 1930, an MA in 1931 and a PhD in 1934, he then published several groundbreaking works, including *The Organism* (1934) and *Motivation and Personality*.

In *Motivation and Personality*, Maslow introduced the original five-stage hierarchy of needs. Often depicted as a pyramid, the model showed that while most people progressed up a hierarchy of needs, few ever reached total achievement. The inevitability of being totally happy with one's lot eventually formed a key role in modern-day marketing: businesses constantly offered new and improved products and services to replace existing ones, so consumers were never completely satisfied. Thus businesses kept on profiting from such consumers, who in turn kept on coveting the next best thing.

Play the Maslow game

Rather like an elaborate game of evolution, Maslow's original model suggested that people were motivated by primeval instincts. As a gamer, the marketer's role was to lift people—the characters in the game—to increasingly higher levels of sophistication.

1. Physiological needs

This level was equivalent to a primordial swamp. Initially hardly any products or services were marketed; instead, consumers were more concerned with having basics like oxygen, water, protein and vitamins. They needed rest, reassurance and freedom to perform simple tasks. Maslow believed a shortage of even one of these essentials led consumers to search for survival solutions. So, for example, a lack of vitamin A would encourage consumers to seek out foods like milk. It was up to marketing soul traders to ensure that their brand of milk became the consumers' natural choice.

2. Safety and security needs

At the second level the central character evolves into Consumer Man (CM), concerned with protection and security. Fear of the menacing unknown was never far away. In real life, soul traders knew and capitalized on such qualms.

For example, in 2008 an ever more congested planet meant consumers felt insecure because of looming social menaces like local knife-wielding gangs. The media continuously warned about recession and job insecurity. Such fears created a general sense of social unease. As a consequence consumers became obsessed with having essential comforts like homes in safe neighborhoods, steady jobs and insurance. All such concerns offered soul traders a wealth of opportunity to market products or services offering environmentally and ethically sound benefits that promised to keep consumers safe and secure.

3. Love and belonging needs

With Consumer Man's physiological and safety needs addressed, the consumer was relaxed enough to pursue friendships at school, in social groups and of course at work. To avoid ending up loveless and lonely, CM developed relationships both in communities and at work. During the early part of the twenty-first century this was partly achieved by CM joining heavily branded social networking sites such as Facebook.

4. Esteem needs

Soul traders in the 1970s realized the implications of consumer self-esteem. The 1960s had already proved that without it people became bitter and resentful. Maslow spoke of two classes of self-esteem: lower and higher. Esteem at the lower level was concerned with the respect of others; this was the very masculine drive for status, fame, glory, recognition, status, gratitude, dignity, pride, and authority. The higher type involved the need for self-respect, including having confidence, self-determination, and free will. Once this was achieved, everything else fell into line.

New consumer-empowering innovations like the Barclaycard credit card, which was introduced in 1966, utilized the concept of self-respect by giving the power to buy goods on a whim without actually having to carry money. While plastic offered confidence, sociologists warned marketers that if "lower order" needs were swept under the carpet, people would stop caring about fulfilling their potential. But perversely, soul traders saw this as an excuse to sell even more products and services positioned to offer consumers an increased sense of self worth, through the owning of things intended to make them feel complete.

5. The final original level: self-actualization

Maslow called the first four levels deficit needs, or "D-needs." If CM had fewer products and services than expected, he felt incomplete and so discontented. The American social psychologist Erich Fromm observed in his book *Beyond the Chains of Illusion: My Encounter with Marx and Freud*, that:

> "We see the world as possessions and potential possessions. Success is a question of how well we can sell ourselves, package ourselves and advertise our values. Our upbringing, education, fashion sense; all are components of an advertisement that is our life."

Maslow called issues related to the final level either "growth motivation" (as opposed to deficit motivation), "being needs" (or "B-needs," in contrast to "D-needs"), or "self-actualization." The last level of Maslow's hierarchy of needs was all about seizing the moment, achieved through realizing the consumer's complete personal potential. To reach this point, marketers had to ensure that consumers had completed each of the previous four levels.

In keeping with the Marxist philosophy "A man is the one who is much, not the one who has much," Maslow believed that few ever reached the level known as self-actualizer. He named only exceptional historical figures meriting the title, who included Abraham Lincoln, Thomas Jefferson, Albert Einstein, Eleanor Roosevelt, Jane Addams, William James, Albert Schweitzer, Benedict Spinoza, and Aldous Huxley.

Maslow believed that all his named examples were "reality-centered." Each could spot a fake promise from a mile off. They dealt with life's difficulties as problems demanding solutions rather than unassailable brick walls. Self-actualizers enjoyed solitude, and rather than have shallow relationships with many people they cultivated deeper personal relationships with a few close friends and family members. They were independent, creative and religious, relishing every new experience. They had an easy-going sense of humor and appreciated people for what they were—rather than what they appeared to be. They had a sense of humility and respect towards others—a trait Maslow called "democratic values." They treasured ethnic and individual variety. They also had "human kinship" (or "Gemeinschaftsgefühl"), social interest, compassion and humanity, all accompanied by strong spiritual ethics. Their only flaws included occasional anxiety, guilt, absentmindedness and excessive kindness, with unexpected flashes of ruthlessness, surgical coldness and loss of humour. None required soul traders, like marketing game players, to manipulate them into feeling contented.

I've always been mad, I know I've been mad,
like the most of us are . . .
very hard to explain why you're mad,
even if you're not mad

Roger Walters, Pink Floyd, "Speak to me"

In the 2000s, Richard Layard, the founder-director of the Centre for Economic Performance at the London School of Economics, made a study of Happiness Economics. He found that income was a poor measure of happiness. If people earned more, but believed others were doing even better, they remained unhappy, feeling that they were just small players in a big rat race. Layard explained that as people became accustomed to higher income levels, their expectations increased, forcing them to work even harder. In the end, the stress of working outstripped the rewards.

Economists have generally assumed that individual preferences are stable. But in reality, argues Layard, thanks in no small part to marketing, which encourages consumers to buy the latest must-have items, the relative value of a person's accumulated possessions has continuously depreciated, as has their sense of happiness. In January 2008, in his book *The Selfish Capitalist*, the eminent clinical psychologist Oliver James pointed out "that not only does market capitalism have little impact on improving happiness, but it actually significantly contributes to certain types of mental illness."

The price of enjoying relatively widespread wealth was stress. Unhappiness among women in Britain almost doubled between 1982 and 2000. Around the time this book was published, the BBC reported that in Britain 300,000 people under the age of 35 were suffering from depression. Despite all the efforts of radicals in the seventies and eighties, selfishness had created a pandemic of low self-esteem driven by a craving for status and celebrity.

Back in the 1970s, it was thought that Maslow's self-actualization could be achieved through an appreciation of beauty, balance and form (reflected in the "teach the world to sing" Coca-Cola commercial). By the mid-1990s, a third edition of Maslow's *Hierarchy of Needs* was published. This time, to achieve complete personal nirvana the consumer had to help others self-actualize. "Give to others to help yourself." Overnight there was a rise in people believing in the right of everyone to believe in anything they liked as long as it was genuinely and freely chosen. Soul traders pitched ideas calculated to be instantly accessible, totally disposable and thoroughly inspiring.

One man was to offer the means to have such high ideals delivered straight onto your lap.

We always overestimate what will change the next two years, and underestimate what will change the next ten

Bill Gates, Chairman of Microsoft Corporation

At 08.01 on June 26, 1974 a checkout girl working at the Marsh supermarket in Troy, Ohio, waved a pack of Wrigley's chewing gum over a scanner. It was the first time in the world that any product was logged with the new computerized system. Seven months later, on January 1, 1975, two young men, one gulping down a Coca-Cola and the other chewing on gum, picked up a copy of *Popular Electronics* magazine. The young men were Bill Gates and Paul Allen. The headline story in the magazine was about MITS (Micro Instrumentation and Telemetry Systems) of Albuquerque, New Mexico, announcing the MITS Altair 8800. Recognizing that the key to the future of personal computing lay in the unlimited potential of software, Gates and Allen set out to adapt BASIC software for the machine.

Working in marathon 24-hour sessions on the Altair's published specifications, Gates and Allen created a simulator on a DEC PDP-10 computer that emulated the MITS machine. The result was the first version of Microsoft BASIC for the Altair.

1975 Microsoft revenue: $16,005. Employees: 3 (Allen, Gates, and Ric Weiland)

By November 1976 the trade name "Microsoft" was registered with the Office of the Secretary of the State of New Mexico "to identify computer programs for use in automatic data processing systems; pre-programming processing systems; and data processing services including computer programming services." In the same year Microsoft developed its first ad campaign, called "The Legend of Micro-Kid." The advert was a four-panel black-and-white cartoon appearing in the microchip journal *Digital Design*. The cartoon's headline read: "Microsoft: What's a microprocessor without it?" The advertising copy explained how Microsoft's range of programming languages could be used to design software that could take advantage of early microprocessors. The cartoon featured a small microchip character—a boxer who had speed and power but grew tired because he lacked training. The other character was a cigar-smoking trainer. The Micro-Kid had a great future but needed the trainer to succeed.

1976 Microsoft revenue: $22,496. Employees: 7

On July 1, 1977, the company shipped its second language, Microsoft's version of Fortran. It started to offer BASIC on a single-copy basis. The company was paid a flat fee of $21,000 for what became Applesoft BASIC. Apple went on to sell more than a million machines with BASIC built in.

1977 Microsoft revenue: $381,715. Employees: 9

In 1978, when Al Gore coined the phrase "information highway," Intel introduced the 8086 chip. Apple co-founder Steve Wozniak wrote Integer BASIC, the first language available for the machine. This was superseded in popularity by Microsoft Applesoft BASIC.

1978 Microsoft revenue: $1,355,655. Employees: 13

On January 1, 1979, Microsoft moved its offices to Bellevue, Washington from Albuquerque, New Mexico. On June 18, Microsoft announced Microsoft BASIC for the 8086 16-bit microprocessor. This was the first release of a resident high-level language for use on 16-bit machines.

On November 29, Microsoft ventured into the European market with the addition of a new representative, Vector Microsoft of Belgium. Microsoft established contracts with ICL, Phillips, R2E, and several others.

1979 Microsoft revenue: $2,390,145. Employees: 28

In 1980 the company introduced Microsoft SoftCard. This made it possible to run programs designed for the CP/M operating system on the Apple II. In the same year Microsoft announced the Microsoft Z-80 SoftCard, a microprocessor that plugged in to the Apple II computer, allowing with only minor modifications for users to run thousands of programs available on the 8080/Z-80 class of computers.

Microsoft also announced Microsoft XENIX OS, a portable operating system designed for 16-bit microprocessors, a multi-user, multi-tasking system running on Intel 8086, Zilog Z8000, Motorola M68000, and the DEC PDP-11 series.

1980 Microsoft revenue: $7,520,720. Employees: 40

Revenue year ending June 30, 2008: $60.42 billion. Bill Gates' wealth: $58 billion (Forbes list 2008)

The PC had become such a ubiquitous part of life that for many the PC became the emblem of Personal Choice.

15

If I ruled the world

Don't be told what you want.
Don't be told what you need.
There's no future for you.

Sex Pistols, "God Save the Queen"

Ronald Reagan and Margaret Thatcher were masters of media manipulation who carried the banner of privatization. He was the wise, witty uncle figure who turned experience of acting in the movies to addressing the world stage. She was an agent of change, the first British woman prime minister and someone who promised not to turn back to old establishment thinking.

They used every classic ploy in the book to assert authority and strengthen their political positions. But their greatest strengths were the people behind the scenes. In Britain, two brothers, a photographer, and a patch of grass in northwest London proved that given the right camera angle, propaganda could make just about any proposition seem truthful. In America government policy was helped along by an invasion and a comic book.

This was a new Garden of Eden where inside even the juiciest apple lay a worm.

Capitalism was the last thing that punk rockers respected. They were the cultural progeny of underground rock. Shaved locks on the sides of their heads left a wave of sticky, greased-up, garishly colored peaks. With safety pins pierced through noses and ears, torn clothing on their backs and bottles of beer tossed into the gutters, the punks pogo-danced against conformity.

It would have been easy to believe that the world of marketing had degenerated into complete anarchy. However, rather than throw in the towel it dawned on marketers that the very passion that had sent the spitting rabble into a frenzy could serve to create a new group of consumers. Soul traders stood on the edge of the mid-1980s and 1990s plotting to mix up a different kind of propaganda cocktail, best served neat on a "grab and run" basis rather than on the rocks.

Towards the end of the 1970s, Jeffrey Bell, an American Vietnam War veteran, decided to turn his talent for writing into a business. He had learned his craft the hard way, writing a speech back in 1975 for Ronald Reagan. The speech backfired; Reagan had lost the New Hampshire primary. Years later Bell reconsidered how Reagan, now running for president, would deliver his message to a worldwide CNN-viewing audience. In 1980 Bell presented his boss with a speech entitled, "Let the People Rule." Somewhat indirectly echoing a speech delivered back in 1963 by Martin Luther King, it promised to free the American people not from the injustice of slavery and racism but from the injustice of a centralized government bloated by excessive bureaucracy. In the speech Reagan proposed "nothing less than a systematic transfer of authority and resources to the states—a program of creative federalism for America's third century."

This time the speech went down well, not just in New Hampshire but in too, where the country's first woman prime minister, the daughter of a grocer from the Lincolnshire town of Grantham, had just made herself a well-deserved cup of tea in 10 Downing Street. Both Thatcher's and Reagan's advisers had been told by SRI that in order to sway the public they had to secure the vote of the "inner directives" who, while being socially aware, were more concerned with looking after themselves. Such insight epitomised the 1980s consumer: outwardly caring, inwardly selfish.

SRI's ideas were also well known to Charles and Maurice Saatchi, who were considered to be the hottest talents in the London advertising industry. Way back in 1971 free love had been acceptable for many people; however, high libidos had led to a higher rate of conception and the Saatchi brothers were asked to come up with a "cool" warning against the consequences of a "hot" sex life. They devised an advert for the Health Education

Council promoting the use of the contraceptive pill. In the poster a doleful-eyed young man, photographed by Alan Brooking, appeared pregnant. With the man looking directly at the reader, the caption said: "Would you be more careful if it was you that got pregnant?" The government loved the unfussy abruptness of the brothers' advert. By the time Margaret Thatcher campaigned for a new election, it seemed an obvious choice to court the Saatchi brothers again.

It was just my imagination running away with me . . .
The Temptations, hit from 1971

The brothers pitched the Tories the idea of a poster showing an endless queue of thousands of people waiting their turn at an unemployment office. Cleverly playing on words, the poster's headline read: "Labour isn't working," with the tag line "Britain's better off with the Conservatives." As with the pregnant man, the razor-sharp bluntness of the concept scored a deep impression with the public. The poster also marked the beginnings of the sound-bite culture, in which laconic, incisive headlines and quotations, rather than drawn-out lengthy arguments, won the day and summed up the moment.

However, on closer examination, the poster was not all it seemed. Back when the campaign was first commissioned, my brother Raphael Gabay was a Conservative councillor for Brent North in London. The local Conservative Member of Parliament, Rhodes Boyson, contacted Raphael to help the party with an important, highly hush-hush project. Boyson explained that the Saatchi brothers needed to photograph at least hundreds, if not thousands, of people for the "Labour isn't working" poster. Raphael was to recruit as many people as possible to turn up for the shoot, which would take place at night on an open field near Wembley. Always keen, Raphael and other Conservative Party workers did what they could. At the time I was about 17 years old. Like most teenagers back then I was more concerned with watching TV programs like *Top of the Pops* than worrying about dull politics.

On a chilly night my brother gave me a lift in his car to the venue on Fryent Way in Wembley. There an agency photographer balanced on a ladder asked the crowd to line up for the shot. The only problem was that, apart from me, only about 20 people had actually turned up. The photographer had to clone us all several times over, quite a feat considering that these were the days before Photoshop had been invented. Look at the poster and somewhere in that queue of "unemployed" you can spot me—several times over—patiently waiting to get back home to watch *Top of the Pops*. I later fulfilled an early ambition by working at Saatchi & Saatchi as one of their Creative Group Heads of Direct Marketing—a job title that, like that poster, appeared far more sophisticated than it actually was!

The sheer nerve of "Labour isn't working" typified the 1980s' "just do it" approach to life. Dan Weiden, the co-founder of advertising agency Wieden and Kennedy, devised that slogan for Nike in 1988. Reflecting this ethic, Margaret Thatcher once said, "Plan your work for today and every day, then work your plan." Like any powerful leader, Thatcher asserted herself and by implication her people.

Argentina

In 1982 Britain found itself at war with Argentina. This was a perfect propaganda opportunity. The Argentinians illegally landed on the British Falkland Islands, planting the Argentine flag in what was British territory. Sending in British troops, Thatcher resurrected mainstream propaganda techniques unseen since World War II. In 1986, news channels showed a scarf- and goggle-clad Prime Minister Thatcher sitting in the turret of a

Challenger tank, resembling (as noted at the time by the *Daily Telegraph*) "a cross between Isadora Duncan, the tempestuous American dancer of the early twentieth century, and Lawrence of Arabia."

The popular Conservative-supporting *Sun* newspaper ran headlines such as "Gotcha!" above a photograph of the Argentine ship the *General Belgrano*, which had been sunk by a British submarine. Other headlines included "Argy Jets Shot Down!," "Our Planes Blitz Argy Ships!," and "Panicky Argies Flee Barefoot!" Proudly revelling in all the propaganda, the *Sun* even produced a T-shirt featuring their slogan: "Stick It Up Your Junta!" The prime minister chastised any media not complying with the propaganda; their crime was seen as the "inappropriate explanation of Britain's case in the Falklands."

Thatcher's rhetoric frequently drew on Britain's celebrated history. She evoked Churchill, drawing on his "British bulldog spirit" and refusal to appease dictators. It was all so reminiscent of classic propaganda spins including demonizing the enemy, glittering generality, expert blessing and card stacking (see pages 101–113).

Perhaps not wishing to be left out in the cold, Thatcher's great ally across the Atlantic also spotted a confidence-building opportunity to turn "jaw-jaw" into a conquest for the electorate's admiration.

Grenada

In 1974 the British discharged their rule over Grenada. One year later Sir Eric Gairy claimed success in a general election. However, the opposition party claimed that the victory was illegitimate. By 1979, working with the opposition forces, the New Jewel Movement launched an armed revolution and overthrew the government. Opting to make alliances with Cuba and other communist states, the new party banned all elections.

In 1983, Reagan was president of America and Grenada had begun work on an international airport that was first proposed by the British as far back as 1954. Pointing to the long runway and oil storage tanks, President Reagan contended that the facility was unnecessary for commercial flights. He said that the airport was probably being built as a Cuban–Soviet airbase, and that made it a potential threat to America. On October 25 Reagan sent 7,000 troops to Grenada, the invasion played well with the press back home in America, and within a few months of the attack *Time* magazine reported the intervention as being a great success.

In addition to sending in armed forces, Reagan put his premier team of perception managers, the CIA, on the project. Thanks to their efforts, Reagan distributed propaganda comics to the Grenadians. The comic featured the American forces coming to heal the plight of the Grenadians. It included scenes such as a communist teacher giving a class of sympathizers the instructions:

- Create fear
- Wipe out opposition
- Bomb schools and buses
- Wreck the economies
- Accuse democracy of all failures
- Create refugee problems

Even George Bush Senior appeared in the comic. The comic's cover showed islanders in 1979 being pistol-whipped by Cuban communists and then, as liberated people in 1983, holding banners thanking American troops.

Why 1984 won't be like "1984"

And the people under the sky were also very much the same—everywhere, all over the world, hundreds or thousands of millions of people just like this, people ignorant of one another's existence, held apart by walls of hatred and lies, and yet almost exactly the same, people who had never learned to think but were storing up in their hearts and bellies and muscles the power that would one day overturn the world.

George Orwell, *1984*

Thanks to computerization, in addition to allowing manufacturers to "just do it," now goods could be manufactured "just in time," producing just enough goods off the production line to meet actual market demand. Even paying for goods followed a "just in time" principle. Whereas in the early sixties and seventies cash in your pocket was the fundamental key to purchasing opportunities, by 1979 Access and Barclaycard credit cards were so popular that they became part of a larger international network of MasterCard and Visa. Consumers simply put their purchases "on the card."

Both the American and the British people were on top of the world. Rather than turning out to be the predicted Orwellian nightmare, brands like Apple Computers set out to ensure that the year 1984 would be a landmark for consumer prosperity. Chiat/Day, Apple's advertising agency, commissioned Ridley Scott to produce an epic futuristic commercial. The new Apple commercial featured a woman athlete wielding a large hammer, with sinister security guards chasing her. The nimble athlete races past armies of dumbstruck people seated in a vast auditorium listening to their leader from a huge screen. The leader is none other than Big Brother himself; the tyrant is celebrating the anniversary of the "Information Purification Directives," which he maniacally summarizes as an end to "contradictory thoughts." Appearing like the Führer addressing a Nazi rally attended by clones of bald-headed people, Big Brother proclaims: "our 'Unification of Thoughts' is more powerful a weapon than anything else . . . We shall prevail." At this the heroine hurls the hammer at the screen. In a flash of light and smoke, the screen, along with Big Brother's sinister image, is obliterated. The commercial ended with a scrolling block of text reading:

"On January 24,
Apple Computer
will introduce Macintosh,
and you'll see
why 1984 won't be like '1984'."

The portability and innovation of the first Macintosh epitomized the freedom of choice offered to consumers. Both Apple and consumers had started on a journey to overthrow the old order. For Apple, at first that journey would be hard. A quarter of a century further down the road, its destination proved to be more than worth all the effort for the brand.

For consumers of products like computers, time was money and there really was no time like the present. In 1986, to borrow a popular phrase from a British TV comedy character of the time, it seemed that just about everyone "had loadsamoney" and, as in the late Leslie Crowther's famous TV catchphrase, everyone was willing "to come on down" because the price was right.

Saatchi & Saatchi's advertising agency group had become the biggest in the world. Consumers were blanket-bombed with advertising reassuring them that life could be a champagne cocktail of exuberance and success. Long-term job security was exchanged for short-term job-hopping. If people needed more money, rather than wait for management to offer modest pay rises, workers simply hopped up the career ladder to another company. This was the age of the YUPPIE—the Young Urban Professional, or Young Upwardly-Mobile Professional. Writing in a 1985 issue of the *Wall Street Journal*, Theresa Kersten at SRI described yuppies as people who fitted the demographic profile, yet expressed resentment of the label: "You're talking about a class of people who put off having families so they can make payments on the BMW."

It's morning again in America

Presidential slogan for Ronald Reagan, 1984

Spin doctors, including those working for politicians like Reagan and Thatcher, re-engineered brands. They convinced the electorate and marketplace alike that common individuals, rather than privileged authorities alone, called the shots. Anyone had the right to be a J. R. Ewing or Alexis Carrington, characters from the 1980s hit TV series *Dallas* and *Dynasty*, wheeling and dealing to secure a future on their terms. Rather than being content to sell consumers small-time Fast Moving Goods such as chocolates, it was time for soul traders to repackage entire state-run utilities and big business corporations.

In Britain, British Gas was privatized. With great aplomb a nationwide marketing campaign aimed at ordinary members of the public was launched with posters, TV commercials, direct mail and advertisements urging the nation that "If you see Sid, tell him" about the launch. On December 8, 1986, British Gas shares were floated on the London stock market. The initial public offering of 135p per share valued the company at £9 billion, at the time the highest equity offering ever. Further large institutions followed suit, and by 2008 many of Britain's leading power organizations were controlled by companies with shareholders outside Britain. These included the French-owned EDF Energy, which controlled a significant percentage of the country's electricity supply.

16

Smoke gets in your eyes

Evidence is now available to indicate that the 14- to 18-year-old group is an increasing segment of the smoking population. RJR-T must soon establish a successful new brand in this market if our position in the industry is to be maintained over the long term.

Planned Assumptions and Forecast for the Period 1977–86 for R. J. Reynolds Tobacco Company, stamped "SECRET," March 15, 1976

Towards the end of the 1980s, consumers became increasingly aware of the dangers of smoking cigarettes. Until then some tobacco companies appeared not only to promote cigarettes as a fashionable part of life but as a right of passage—especially for the very young. Before progressing further through the decades, step behind the bikesheds of time for a sneaky fag and a glimpse into a era when Hollywood glamor, advertised truth and healthy living became a smoke screen for profits and the abuse of society's most easily influenced.

During the 1980s everyone was in the money and it seemed that just about anyone could be exploited. That included preteenagers playing at being grown-up by smoking R. J. Reynolds' Camel brand of cigarettes. In their ads, R. J. Reynolds featured a cartoon camel called Joe. He appeared as cool as the Fonz from the hit TV series *Happy Days*. Throughout his term as the product endorser, the slick-looking Joe posed in everything from swimwear to smart suits and casual jackets. For kids, here was the fun embodiment of the man about town. Many assumed that Joe was aimed at encouraging boys to take up smoking. R. J. Reynolds denied this, saying that the campaign was primarily directed at males aged 25–49 who smoked other brands, in particular Marlboro. In 1974, a memo by the R. J. Reynolds Research Department pointed out that capturing the young-adult market was essential because:

"Most smokers begin smoking regularly and select a usual brand at or before the age of 18 . . . Over 50 percent of men smokers start smoking fairly regularly before the age of 18."

Using cartoons

At a quick glance the Joe Camel character looked innocuous, but there was more to Joe than first met the eye. His nose and mouth resembled a flaccid penis and large scrotum. The image even caught the notice of the rock band Patsy Division, which paid homage to the posters with the song "Touch My Joe Camel":

I saw the billboard and thought of you.
Low hanging balls, round and smooth.
I don't smoke, ain't gonna start—
Just 'cause they made public a private part.
They give pleasure, let there be no doubt.
I like having one in my mouth.
I want to touch your Joe Camel
I want to touch your Joe Camel
And while we're at it, reach out and grab it.

The American public was outraged—not by Joe's well-endowed facial qualities—but the use of a cartoon to attract children to smoking. In reality Camel wasn't even the first cigarette brand to exploit children; the original Flintstones cartoon series showed Fred Flintstone and his best friend, Barney Rubble, puffing on the series sponsor's brand of cigarettes—Winston.

Chesterfield ran a commercial aimed at children discussing "the Chesterfield King." In the commercial, a hippy-sounding king (voiced-over by Daws Butler, who also provided the voice for Huckleberry Hound, Yogi Bear, Snagglepuss and Muttley) says:

"Does thou swear to enjoy the Chesterfield King; the king that has everything?" A suitably groovy knight replies, 'I doth appreciate Chesterfield's big, big length, like you know—and the smoothest taste and the smoothest natural tobacco filter of any king . . . you know what I mean."

Even Marlboro had an animated commercial. It featured a couple of hapless characters called Harry and Juggernaut Jones, who acted similarly to Jack Lemmon and Walter Matthau in the 1968 classic *The Odd Couple*. Harry and Juggernaut had a friendly banter about Marlboro cigarettes whilst a catchy jingle sang: "You get a lot to like in a Marlboro—filter, flavor, pack or box."

By April 1970, Congress had passed the Public Health Cigarette Smoking Act, which banned the advertising of cigarettes on TV and radio. After 1971, most tobacco advertising appeared in magazines and newspapers and on billboards. Since the introduction of the Federal Cigarette Labeling and Advertising Act all packaging and advertisements had to display a health warning from the Surgeon General. The last cigarette commercial on American TV was aired on January 1, 1971.

R. J. Reynolds first highlighted their products in comic-strip form back in 1938, with strips featuring "One day in the life of Jimmie Lynch—daredevil test driver." Decades later it was finally time to smooth over issues. The company published full-page advertisements with the headline, "Let's Clear the Air on Smoking," stating that smoking was an adult habit. The company was right: by then some of the children affected by the original 1970s Joe Camel advertisements were old enough to freely choose their favorite brand of cigarettes.

Paying for product placement

As early as the release of the first sound movie in 1927, the tobacco industry ensured that products attracted star billing. During the golden era of Hollywood, from 1930–40, R. J. Reynolds along with American Tobacco and Liggett & Meyers paid at least 200 Hollywood stars millions of dollars to smoke on the silver screen. A-list stars included two-thirds of the top 50 box-office actors, such as Gary Cooper, Clark Gable, Joan Crawford, Spencer Tracy, Bob Hope and Henry Fonda.

According to the British magazine *Tobacco Control,* John Wayne was particularly dependent on the sponsored cigarettes. He eventually died of cancer. In addition to convincing the stars that cigarettes aided relaxation and improved their voice, in 1937–38 alone, American Tobacco paid $218,750 ($3.2 million dollars in today's prices) to promote Lucky Strike. Part of the brand strategy behind Lucky Strike was to get the cigarette into the consciousness of the general public. With this in mind, the Lucky Strike jingle was continuously played over the radio. On one occasion the jingle was broadcast 268 consecutive times on a radio show that lasted only 135 minutes.

In Britain, stars like Sid James, who appeared in many *Carry On* movies, frequently supplemented their wages by making deals with companies such as Johnny Walker to get their products featured in scenes.

Today, brands are prepared to pay millions of dollars to have their products featured in box-office hits featuring established characters like James Bond. In *Die Another Day*, 20 companies paid £44m to have their products shown on screen or to use the Bond brand in advertising. For *Quantum of Solace*, Sony paid the movie's producers to feature everything from Sony computers to TV screens, cellphones and handycams; Ford and Aston Martin cars, along with Omega watches, were also featured. Coca-Cola produced a series of advertisements that linked their product Coke Zero with the movie; Virgin Airways paid to have Bond fly Upper Class on one of their transatlantic routes; and luxury private-jet manufacturer Ocean Sky invested around $190 million alone in multiple product placements in the movie.

In 1991, following the public concern years earlier regarding Joe Camel, the *Journal of the American Medical Association* published a study that suggested more children aged five and six years could recognize Joe Camel than Mickey Mouse or Fred Flintstone—bad news for Winston cigarettes.[6]

In addition to encouraging children to smoke, it was commonplace in the seventies for publishers of comics featuring harmless characters, like Casper the Friendly Ghost or Marvel superheroes, to accept advertising from companies selling products such as cigarette lighters with the headline: "The 'all-in-one' cigarette light and full pack case—personalized with your name." As if cigarettes weren't enough, comics aimed at children under ten years old even carried advertisements for lethal weapons such as the "Automatic Firing Tripod Machine Gun," which fired ten rounds of BB bullets at a time.

The German woman does not smoke!

Nazi anti-smoking slogan

England was the first country with a leader who pointed out the health hazards of smoking. In 1604, King James I delivered a treatise called *A Counterblaste to Tobacco*. King James noted that smoking was: "A custome lothsome to the eye, hatefull to the Nose, harmfull to the braine, dangerous to the Lungs, and in the blacke stinking fume thereof, nearest resembling the horrible Stigian smoke of the pit that is bottomelesse."

The first European country to try to ban smoking officially was Germany under Nazi rule. At the time a popular Nazi magazine published:

"Brother National Socialist, do you know that our Führer is against smoking and thinks that every German is responsible to the whole people for all his deeds and emissions, and does not have the right to damage his body with drugs?"[7]

The Nazis restricted tobacco advertising, and banned smoking in most public buildings. They restricted and regulated tobacco farmers' growing abilities, and even had a sophisticated anti-smoking public relations campaign. Hitler gave a gold watch to commanders who quit the habit. Reichsführer Heinrich Himmler banned SS men from smoking on duty. Goebbels hid his cigarettes in front of movie crews.

Nazi-supported anti-tobacco activists banned smoking from government offices, civic transport, university campuses, rest homes, post offices, many restaurants and bars, hospital grounds and workplaces. Tobacco taxes were raised, unsupervised cigarette vending machines were banned, and there were calls for a ban on smoking while driving.

They think it's all over . . .

In the 1980s smoking was costing countries dearly. In Britain alone 114,000 were dying each year from cigarette-related illnesses. In 1999 the American Federal Trade Commission suggested that cigarette manufacturers spent $8.24 billion on advertising and promotion. Marketing consultants A. C. Nielsen announced that during the period September 2001 to August 2002, tobacco companies in Britain had spent £25 million on advertising, broken down as follows:

£11 million on press advertising
£13.2 million on posters
£714,550 on radio advertising
£106,253 on direct-mail advertising

By July 2005, a EU directive banned cigarette advertising in countries where tobacco marketing remained a huge business. During June 2008, the BBC reported that British American Tobacco (BAT) broke its own marketing code covering the sale of cigarettes to young people in Africa. In Malawi, a BBC TV report by the self-made millionaire Duncan Bannatyne found evidence of BAT providing sponsorship at a music event where celebrities wore Embassy- and Pall Mall-branded goods and which opened its doors to under-age smokers. Bannatyne also found evidence of children being sold single cigarettes. BAT's own marketing code acknowledged that single cigarettes (known as "sticks") were particularly attractive to young people, unable to afford a whole packet of cigarettes. Chris Proctor, Head of Science and Regulation at BAT, said: "If that was the case, that is disappointing; it's certainly not what we would wish to happen."

In Mauritius, Bannatyne discovered special pots distributed to shops by BAT to make it more convenient to sell "sticks." In Malawi and Nigeria, he found posters produced by BAT featuring the price of a single cigarette. Responding to Bannatyne's findings, Chris Proctor said existing posters advertising single sticks would not be used after June 2008.

BAT also decorated shops in the same color as one of their branded cigarettes, "Matinee." One shopkeeper told Bannatyne that his shop had been painted three years earlier by BAT in order to advertise its cigarettes, even though a local ban on advertising cigarettes was introduced in 1999.

In 2008 the World Health Organization (WHO) estimated that the number of smoking-related deaths in Africa was 100,000 a year, a figure that was predicted to double over the next 20 years.

17

Make love not death

Sometimes I have a terrible feeling that I am dying not from the virus, but from being untouchable.

Amanda Heggs, AIDS sufferer, quoted in the *Guardian*, June 12, 1989

The discovery of AIDS was like an earthquake, but one that continues to crack open beneath society's feet with the aftershocks rumbling on through public conscience. Trying to change the human sex drive had to be the most challenging and controversial of all communications campaigns to implement, but during the 1980s some of the most creative talents in the business were ready to pick up the gauntlet. Their ideas not only helped save lives but set the tone for a new, more open society prepared to face previously taboo demons and to accept different lifestyles.

In 1986, the British Deputy Prime Minister, William Whitelaw, had far more pressing issues on his mind than the chronic effects of smoking on public health. He was chairing a Cabinet committee meeting on a disease that did not just threaten the nation's general well-being, but which it was feared could potentially wipe out civilization itself—AIDS.

The government decided to call for help from some old friends, Saatchi & Saatchi, who had recently produced award-winning posters for Silk Cut cigarettes. The posters had been inspired by a Californian valley art installation by Christo and Jeanne-Claude. For psychologists, the posters of a slashed piece of silk echoed the Freudian theory of Thanatos. According to Freud, humans have a life instinct (Eros) and a death instinct (Thanatos), and the latter compels humans to engage in risky and destructive behaviors that could lead to their own death. Psychologists suggested the advert's imagery of cuts alluded to slashing of flesh.

Craving love's touch—dreading death's kiss

Saatchi & Saatchi arranged for leaflets with the slogan: "AIDS—Don't Die of Ignorance" to be posted to 23 million homes in

Britain. A hard-hitting commercial featuring a tombstone with the same headline sent ripples of shock and horror through the country. The script read:

> "There is now a danger that has become a threat to us all. It is a deadly disease and there is no known cure. The virus can be passed during sexual intercourse with an infected person. Anyone can get it, man or woman. So far it's been confined to small groups, but it's spreading. So protect yourself and read this leaflet when it arrives. If you ignore AIDS, it could be the death of you."

It dawned on people that their next sexual act could turn out to be nothing less than a death sentence. The commercial had such an impact that, rather than acting as a warning, it created a sense of restrained but occasionally openly vocalized mass hysteria.

In 1987, the American TV-show host Oprah Winfrey solemnly warned her viewers: "Research studies now project that one in five heterosexuals could be dead from AIDS at the end of the next three years." The American Surgeon General C. Everett Koop referred to the virus as "the biggest threat to health that this nation has ever faced." As the public began to hear that HIV could lead to AIDS, which was prominent in the gay community, it turned against anyone who might be homosexual. Worse still, any straight people with aspirations of "coming out" to an understanding society were soon scuppered. Parodying an S. C. Johnson commercial for Raid insecticide that read "Raid Kills Bugs Dead," anti-gay protestors held banners reading "Aids Kills Fags Dead."

With the passing years it became clear that the threatened "wipeout" of anyone having sex wouldn't come to pass, and people slowly started to ignore the warnings. New commercials and advertisements were introduced to show that the virus, while not uncontrollable, could still infect those who didn't practice safe sex or take sensible precautions with drugs. Advertisements discussed how condoms could help prevent AIDS. They also looked at better hygiene for intravenous drug addicts. Throughout the 1960s and 1970s, the American National Association of Broadcasters (NAB) Code of Conduct prohibited condom advertising outright. However, a Californian TV station violated the prohibition by broadcasting a Trojan condom commercial in 1975. The law was revoked in 1979 after the Justice Department brought an antitrust lawsuit, and in 1991, FOX Broadcasting became the first American network to break the longstanding taboo against paid condom advertising. By 1988 rather than ostracize some members of the community, soul traders concentrated on messages of inclusion. AIDS, like taxes, had become part and parcel of everyday life, which had to be prudently managed rather than aggressively fought. The idea of simply carrying around a discreet box of condoms perfectly suited a sexually promiscuous society. With a packet of three branded condoms in your pocket, even death itself could be contained.

Rather than use scare tactics, governments were advised to win the confidence of those most vulnerable to the virus—the young —by repackaging AIDS as a social cause rather than as a messy disease. Taking up the cause, rock stars belted out songs related to the tragic social consequences of the disease. "We've all lost so many good friends to AIDS" would be a familiar sentiment echoed by performers at AIDS-awareness rock concerts. Just as *Schindler's List* neatly packaged the full horrors of concentration camps into a tearful but ultimately sanitized three hours, so movies like *Philadelphia* brought the AIDS cause to a worldwide audience. TV channels like MTV featured footage from charity and awareness-raising concerts attended by thousands swaying in unison to show solidarity as the generation ready to assume ownership, rather than victimization, of the disease.

Such concerts were punctuated with slickly produced short movies featuring ashen-looking rock stars visiting Africans dying in thousands from the disease. While prompting audiences to feel deeply sympathetic to the plight of such people, the clips made many come to the conclusion that the disaster being played out halfway around the other side of the world was someone else's concern. These problems didn't need individual action but called for the voice of ambassadors and elders from the world of rock and pop—who would speak on behalf of devoted fans. The delegation of responsibilities freed ordinary people to continue having a good time—both in and outside of the music venues.

Before long any rock star wanting to show that they were at one with their fans, and to secure music sales, offered at least one free concert in aid of the great social cause, which by now even had its own branded logo—a red ribbon. Fans seeing their rock idols on the world political stage argue against AIDS or poverty had more than just recording artists to admire. Now they had prophets of popular culture. Such prophets and sibyls from the world of movies, rock, sports and fashion offered marketers perfect celebrity vehicles to endorse products or services.

Although well intentioned, the longer-term effects of this populist tactic in the West exacerbated a sense of ambivalence toward what was, after all, a life-threatening disease. AIDS-awareness concerts eventually became little more than excuses for a great day out to listen to music. Governments had to remind people that the disease was still around. Rather than being a cause taken up by the young alone it needed to be embraced by the whole of society—or even be incorporated into their social psyche. At the start of the 1990s American advertising agency Calet Hirsch & Ferrell ran an advert with the headline: "Baseball, hotdogs, apple pie and AIDS." The main copy read:

"AIDS has become part of our country. Find out how you can help end this American way of life. And death. Call 1-800-342—AIDS."

Back in 1986 when the original "ignorance" campaign was launched, the World Health Organization reported 43,880 cases of AIDS in 91 countries. Thanks to new medical breakthroughs supported by that campaign and others that followed, by the end of 2006 an estimated 73,000 people were living with HIV (as opposed to dying from it). A third were unaware of their infection.

At the time of writing there have been 23,596 diagnoses of actual AIDS in Britain. At least 17,932 people diagnosed with HIV have died, and at least 80 percent of these deaths followed an AIDS diagnosis. The World Health Organization reported in 2007 that 33.2 million people were estimated to be living with the HIV virus, a decrease from 2006 when it was estimated that 39.5 million people were living with HIV. (Source: Centre for Disease Control and Prevention, 2005.)

At the time of writing, 30 million people have no access to HIV treatment and every day 70,000 people worldwide are infected with the virus. According to British-based AIDS group Avert, half of those who acquire HIV are under the age of 25. With diseases like AIDS becoming more socially tolerable, lenience became a byword of the era. Society was more relaxed and people were keen to focus their attention on themselves rather than on any threats to the welfare of the wider society. Such horrors were simply too big to be tackled on an individual basis.

If ever there was an example of living in a house of cards, the 1990s was it. The walls were about to collapse.

18

Emblems of pride and enterprise

People of Berlin—people of the world—this is our moment. This is our time.

Presidential candidate Barack Obama speaking in Berlin, 2008

Margaret Thatcher's impromptu action at a Conservative Party Conference, when she covered up the new British Airways logo on a model aircraft, neatly captured the nation's pride in its flag. From BA's bungled attempt to make its image more international to the ridiculing of the 2012 Olympic logo, the branding and rebranding of Britain's biggest companies has been important to the nation's sense of identity.

Perhaps Günter Schabowski should have taken more time to study the note handed to him in November 1989. Maybe his recent vacation had put him off guard. The note said that in the morning a few East Berliners would be allowed to cross the border between East and West Germany for private travel. Schabowski read it aloud at a press conference, assuming that the borders would immediately be open to everyone. As a result, tens of thousands of East Berliners flooded the checkpoints in the Wall demanding entry into West Berlin. Overwhelmed border guards had little choice but to open the checkpoints, allowing the flood to spread.

Spotting a unique opportunity, Saatchi & Saatchi quickly posted an advertisement on the Berlin Wall: "Saatchi & Saatchi, first over the wall." At 0:00 CET on October 3, 1990, Germany was fully reunified. The opening of the East heralded a completely new group of consumers ready to be introduced to the joys of Western excess.

Flying the flag

No longer prime minister, but still an influential political figure, during the 1997 Tory conference Margaret Thatcher approached a model aircraft from the national airline, British Airways. The airline had just redesigned its logo, at the cost of £60 million. Whipping out her handkerchief she covered the model's tail that showed off the logo, muttering, "We fly the British flag, not these awful things—tape it up."

The new design turned out to be disastrous for British Airways. The rebrand called for the fleet's aircraft tails to be painted in various designs from around the world. Introducing the scheme, BA's Chief Executive Bob Ayling told the press that the design proved that British Airways was international. In this era of globalization, 60 percent of passengers were non-British and some considered the old BA colors "stuffy."

At the time of the fiasco I spoke to Chris Holt, a design manager at British Airways, about the company's whole brand experience. "Part of our marketing strategy is to stretch the brand into an experience beyond just the aircraft seat. After all, the customer encounter with the company isn't simply about sitting in an aeroplane—but either side of that. Stretching the brand is about enhancing the travel experience. Whether it's insurance, medical services, ground transportation, hotels, holidays, theatre tickets, shopping and airport lounges, tailor-made packages for business travellers . . . it all counts. As long as the brand extension is directly related to core—it's worth exploring." While Holt did his best to justify the rebranding exercise, passengers simply wouldn't put up with the idea of losing the original Union Jack logo. Eventually the company was compelled to spend two and half years repainting 170 aircraft.

In 1999 Richard Branson began expanding his own fleet of Virgin aircraft. Spotting a great public relations coup, Branson repainted his planes with the Union Jack colors. "When I talk to people from overseas they feel that Britain is something to be proud of and flying in a British carrier, whether it is Virgin or BA, is something that they feel secure and safe in. The squiggly lines didn't work, in Britain or abroad, and BA's profits have dive-bombed since they introduced them and Virgin's have gone soaring up since we brought the flag back, so I don't think it worked. I think if they asked a few people after they had done the first one or two planes, they most likely would not have done any more," said a patriotic Branson to reporters.[8]

Although not its own fault, British Airways was subjected to a second international brand flop in 2008 when Terminal Five, run exclusively for British Airways at Heathrow Airport, opened with most of its infrastructure totally inoperable. The press went to town condemning British Airways as a brand disaster. Worse still, months after the launch, the British Airports Authority (BAA) admitted that at best, only part of Heathrow East would be open for business in time for the 2012 Olympic Games.

The British 2012 Olympic logo also suffered an identity crisis. Designed by London-based brand consultants Wolff Olins at an estimated cost of £400,000, it was universally ridiculed as a total mess rather than a cohesive brand identity. So poor was its execution that when animated it even had the potential to induce epileptic episodes.

As for British Airways, in 2001 a new senior design manager, Mike Crump, delivered a complete U-turn on any previous management decisions, saying, "Our aim is to bring back consistency and unity to the BA brand through a simpler identity. Research has shown that our core customers and staff worldwide like the Union flag design. They believe it better reflects the direction the company is now heading in and reinforces a core goal of Britishness in a more modern and less formal way."

Mail your packages early so the post office can lose them in time for Christmas.

Johnny Carson, TV host and comedian

In 2001, the UK Post Office Group decided to reposition itself. Research suggested that the brand name was associated with words such as "trust," "honor," and "valor" (delivering the post in all weathers). However, there was also a lot of confusion regarding the roles of its different divisions, such as Royal Mail, local post offices and Parcel Force. The company's managers felt that the organization needed to be positioned as a public limited company operating at arm's length from its sole shareholder—the British government.

So the Post Office's name was altered to Consignia. The branding agency responsible for the change (Dragon) said, "It's got consign in it. It's got a link with insignia, so there is this kind of royalty-ish thing."[9] According to reports, the name change cost the Post Office the regal sum of £2m in modifying stationery, signage and so on. It also cost their credibility. Ordinary users of the Post Office simply didn't understand why the name had to change at all. Most believed it dealt a blow to their British heritage and spelt the ominous end of local government-run community post offices to big corporate giants. Some were confused as to the meaning of the new name, and there were unfortunate resonances; in Spanish, "consignia" meant lost luggage. To compound issues, the brand amendment coincided with industrial disputes and fierce competition and the company reported a record £281m loss for the six months to November 2001.

The entire "logo-gate" affair cost British Airways dearly, but for Margaret Thatcher her patriotic outburst was met with approval from both the electorate and consumers alike, who felt that their sense of identity was being lost through globalization.

19

Food, glorious food

*To eat is a necessity, but to eat intelligently
is an art*

La Rochefoucauld, seventeenth-century French writer

The end of the Cold War heralded a new appetite for Western culture. Thanks to shrewd campaigns, supersized economies suddenly offered soul traders new opportunities. It was the era of the fast-food economy. Everyone wanted to supersize their consumption of the good life. Consumers were addicted to snacking on feel-good treats that bloated the food industry's profits. The new emergence of Eastern Europe not only gave marketers a bigger appetite for exporting global brands like hamburgers, it also opened the doors to a new outpost from where old enemies would emerge as new contenders in the race for market share.

In 1991, the USSR was dissolved and, with the Cold War now over, Russia could be seen as 17,075,400 square kilometers of prime marketing space up for grabs. On January 31, 1990, McDonald's opened its first restaurant on Russian soil in Moscow's Pushkin Square, adjusting its menu to include, among other traditional Russian food specialties, cabbage pie. By the mid-2000s, the restaurant was serving 30,000 customers a day. Within ten years of its launch, McDonald's employed over 17,000 Russians and owned a real estate portfolio conservatively valued at $115 million. It had 127 restaurants in 37 Russian cities. By 2008 it had served over one billion customers.

Meanwhile, in the West overweight customers happily gobbled burger after burger as long as they ordered a Diet Coke to wash it all down—convincing themselves they were looking after their health by drinking something that incorporated the word "diet." In marketing, students learn about "anchoring." This occurs when a consumer, having little knowledge of something, chooses a random aspect to "anchor" their decision on. For example, if a point-of-sale campaign reads "20 percent off—now only £9,999," consumers think they must buy it, drawn to the small 20 percent reduction while overlooking the actual huge £9,999 cost.

Where fast food was concerned, many consumers chose to ignore government health warnings about the risks of overeating. In 2007, nearly a quarter of British adults were obese—an increase of 50 percent since 1998, while one in six children between the ages of two and fifteen were categorised as obese. The World Health Organization predicted there would be 2.3 billion overweight adults in the world by 2015.

Six months after spotting this worrying trend, market research firm Synovate questioned 9,000 people in 13 countries across five continents about their attitudes to food. Obesity was blamed on food advertisements. Respondents from Britain and America said they would be unable to give up fast food, pointing to a lack of self-discipline as the main cause of obesity. Forty-four percent of Americans said they would be unable to give up their burgers, pizzas and chicken wings.

In August 2007, researchers at America's Stanford University revealed that children as young as three years old reacted to the "yellow arches" logo of McDonald's, particularly on packaging such as take-out bags. Stanford scientists asked 63 children aged between three and five to take part in over 104 taste tests of some of the burger chain's most popular menu items, including a burger, french fries and chicken nuggets. On average, 48 percent preferred the taste of food pulled out of McDonald's bags to the taste of the same food items from plain paper bags. Thirty-seven percent preferred the unmarked burger and 59 percent liked the McDonald's branded chicken nuggets. Eighteen percent went for the unbranded nuggets and 77 percent said the french fries in the McDonald's bag tasted better than the fries from a plain white bag.

We don't print the truth, we print what we know.
We print what the people tell us and this means we
print lies.

Former president Richard Nixon quoting Ben Bradlee, former managing editor of the
Washington Post, May 1977, interview with David Frost on the issue of Watergate

In 2007, I helped a TV news team with a story regarding salmonella and Cadbury's chocolate. Cadbury, one of the TV station's biggest advertisers, was widely reported to have had traces of salmonella found in their factory. Despite the chocolate being safe to eat, it was a huge story.

The news team conducted a filmed experiment with mothers and young children in a local London park. As you can imagine, working with young children, the filming took much longer than usual to organize. We asked the mums and children to taste a selection of unmarked bars. The kids liked all the sweets; the mums nibbled and nibbled. But once we disclosed that one of the bars was the Cadbury's brand, in a flash, the worried mothers nervously snatched them out of their children's hands. Meanwhile, on seeing the revealed Cadbury's logo, despite previously enjoying all the unmarked bars with equal fervour, the children declared that they would sooner gobble down the bars with the familiar brand name. Frustratingly, despite all the time taken and bars munched, last-second editorial decisions meant that the footage showing shocked mothers snatching branded bars from young mouths was never broadcast.

Back in Russia, parents working as "burger flippers" to feed young children had a tough time. Compared to the West, wages for Russians were much more modest. In 2007, the average income reached 11,000 roubles, or about $420 per month. In Britain, according to the Office of National Statistics, average earnings per month during 2007 were £457 ($909.763). By 2008, UBS AG estimated that the Russian retail food industry was worth $145 billion. It was expected to expand by 17 percent annually through to at least 2010. Marketing's influence on Russia was lucrative. The first of several IKEA superstores in Russia topped $100m in sales during the first year of operation alone in 2000.

Towards the close of the twenty-first century's first decade, Russia no longer worried about being perceived as "the last great marketing outpost." It could stand on its own, sending hundreds of multi-millionaire citizens around the world to call the shots on major marketing brands from the world of sports to the world of finance. According to Forbes, in 2008 Russia had 53 billionaires who were collectively worth a total of $282 billion. A Russian think tank, the Centre for Economic and Financial Research, said the country had 103,000 millionaires, collectively worth $670 billion.

Companies like British Petroleum accused the Kremlin of turning a blind eye to asset grabbing by powerful Russian oligarchs. With the West running out of oil, Russia could call the shots on business and, as a country with rising numbers of impoverished people with guns, it would send a shudder through Western sensibilities.

20

The girl in the ponytail

*If you can fake sincerity, you can fake
pretty much anything*

Dr Greg House, character in the American TV series *House*

Saddam Hussein's invasion of Kuwait in 1990 posed a huge problem for America. Kuwait was one of the richest nations on earth and its people were keen supporters of American interests. The White House wanted to gain public approval for American military support of Kuwait and it turned to the PR industry for help, which turned to a 15-year-old Kuwaiti girl to artfully produce a tearful plea. Her televized performance helped to bring grown men to tears and nations to the theatre of war.

Khamzat Khasbulatov had progressed up the career ladder to serve as McDonald's President of Russia, Ukraine and Belarus. He would have been just the kind of executive deeply affected by CNN's 1990 24-hour coverage of American soldiers being air-dropped near Kuwait's Iraqi border.

Only eight days prior to the attack, Saddam Hussein had been given tacit approval of his plans by the American Ambassador to Iraq, April Glaspie, who said America took ". . . no position in the event of any border conflict between Iraq and Kuwait." Since his botched-up attempt back in 1959 to assassinate the Iraqi Prime Minister, Abdul Karim Qassim, Saddam had played a useful role for America and Britain, including signing Iraq up to the anti-Soviet Baghdad Pact. Following the loss of their foothold in India, the deal offered the British a means to retain some degree of control in the Middle East. Saddam had become increasingly self-assured and assertive, believing that at last it was he who controlled the strings rather than any foreign masters.

Until then both the American and the British public had had a rose-colored view of their Middle Eastern ally, albeit a very faint tint of rose. In 1969, the British embassy in Baghdad described Saddam as "the recognized heir-apparent," as "young" with an "engaging smile" and "a formidable, single-minded and hard-headed member of the Ba'athist hierarchy, but one with whom, if only one could see more of him, it would be possible to do business."[10] By the early 1990s, Saddam was looking for funds to support his regime. The Iran–Iraq war had left the country financially crippled, with a war debt of roughly $75 billion. The Kuwaitis refused to help, leaving Saddam to ask America for funds, something that would do nothing to enhance his public image with Arab neighbours.

Using the excuse that the Kuwaiti monarchy had slant-drilled oil from wells which Iraq considered to be within its border, and taking the lead from Ambassador Glaspie's comments, Saddam forged ahead with his invasion. Iraq left America with no other option than to intervene, summoning up a coalition of forces to come to the aid of the Kuwaitis. But pitching a justification to the American people for the intervention wasn't going to be easy for political soul traders. At the time, Craig Fuller headed the Washington office of Hill & Knowlton; the company was paid $10 million to help shape public perceptions of the war.

On October 10, some two months into the conflict, a pretty 15-year-old Kuwaiti girl wearing her hair in a ponytail quietly told a committee of men and women from the United States Congressional Human Rights Caucus about Saddam's cruelty to her people. She explained that she had worked as a volunteer in the Al-Idar hospital: "While I was there, I saw the Iraqi soldiers come into the hospital with guns. They took the babies out of the incubators and left the children to die on the cold floor." Hearing this, and reportedly on the verge of tears, the Chair of the Committee Tom Lathos bit his quivering bottom lip.

In the following weeks, White House speechwriters ensured that the 15-year-old's description of babies being pulled from incubators and scattered like firewood across the floor would be constantly referred to by the President. At the time few thought to dig deeper into the identity of the girl, known only as Nayirah. After all, according to "Citizens for a Free Kuwait," which had persuaded her to deliver the testimonial, the poor girl needed to protect her family back home. In fact it wasn't just her full name that "Citizens for a Free Kuwait" kept quiet about; it turned out that little Nayirah was the daughter of Saud bin Nasir Al-Sabah, a Kuwaiti ambassador and part of the fabulously rich and austere Kuwaiti royal family.

Hill & Knowlton managed "Citizens for a Free Kuwait," and Nayirah's accounts of the mass incubator slaughters were never independently confirmed. As the Congressional Human Rights Caucus meeting had no statutory basis, no one could be prosecuted for perjury. However, on discovering the full facts, Amnesty International retracted its support.

Yet Kuwait and its people did indeed suffer tremendous losses as a result of the Iraqi invasion. No fewer than 700 oil fields were set ablaze by retreating Iraqi forces, around six million barrels of oil a day were lost during the war, and the effect on the surrounding environment was catastrophic. In addition to helping to clean up the oil slicks, American companies were recruited to polish up Kuwait's image as a non-democratic state and by 2008 Kuwait was considered by the West to be one of the most democratic states in the Middle East.[11]

Another PR company, the Rendon Group, had helped tidy up a few problems following the CIA's involvement in the overthrow of General Noriega in Panama during 1989. Like Saddam Hussein, General Noriega was formerly on the CIA's payroll. Noriega was discovered to be a double agent and was sentenced to serve a long term in prison for trafficking and money laundering. The Rendon Group had advised Noriega's opponent on managing his public image.

In 1990, the Rendon Group was tasked by Kuwait with a job described by the *Washington Post* as:

"Deflecting attention away from the controversial aspects of the country; the lack of a democratic system of government, treatment of women as second-class citizens, the flamboyant lifestyle of some members of the Kuwaiti elite and a predilection for leaving all nuts-and-bolts work to foreign guest workers."

Between the invasion and the end of the war, Kuwait reportedly paid an estimated $770,000 to the Rendon Group, as well as $20,000 to Pintak-Brown International, a Washington-based public relations group which allegedly distributed a book called *Kuwait on the March*. Kuwait also paid $1 million towards the cost of producing the book *The Rape of Kuwait: The True Story of Iraqi Atrocities Against a Civilian Population*. Further payments were also made to the lobby group of Neill and Co., which received $150,000, and the law firm of Cleary, Gottlieb, Steen & Hamilton, which received $1.7 million.[12]

According to Solomon Hughes in *War on Terror, Inc.*, the Rendon Group also organized 20,000 Valentine's Day cards to be sent to American troops along with thousands of small American flags to be waved at columns of American troops driving triumphantly into Kuwait City.

Once the war was finally over the CNN effect meant that the real victors turned out to be the TV audiences watching the whole episode unfold. Their taste for powerful images from the battlefield encouraged companies to market computer war games that could be played even by kids on school-bus runs.

21

Everyone clicks
with someone

You affect the world by what you browse

Tim Berners-Lee, inventor of the World Wide Web

In the early 1990s, Tim Berners-Lee's radical invention of the World Wide Web led the world into a whole new era. The possibilities of the internet for information, communication and business were literally endless, and among the first to realize the extent of its promise was the sex industry. It lured a vast audience, who were drawn in through the apparent safety and anonymity of their home computers. Such an audience offered rich opportunities for the spiders weaving their pornographic webs. Their potential profits were obscenely large.

––––––––––

Tim was a child genius obsessed with mathematics. He viewed the world not just in three dimensions, but through the eyes of an insightful mathematician. By the time he reached 34 his highly original insights into advanced mathematics had landed him a job at the European Laboratory for Particle Physics, more popularly known as CERN. Here he proposed a new protocol for information distribution. In 1991 this protocol became the World Wide Web. It was based on hypertext, a system of embedding links in text to link to other text. The breakthrough turned out to be one of mankind's most important discoveries. In the long term it helped restore business confidence in Tim Berners-Lee's homeland, Britain, which in 1992, under the governance of the newly elected Conservative Party led by John Major, plunged into a deep recession. It also formed the foundations of a completely new economy that wasn't even part of the bricks-and-mortar world. Through technological advances marketed to the ordinary person in the street, Tim's protocol redefined how people worked, lived and played.

Everyone wanted to hitch a ride on the World Wide Web. That trip had to be smooth and efficient. In March 1993, Intel introduced the Pentium microprocessor. Huge amounts of data could be processed in seconds, giving computer manufacturers the opportunity to sell mass-produced computers to consumers.

Meeting the demand for virtual shop windows, technical geeks became web designers. At first most corporate sites were little more than a series of hypertext links about corporate information, but soon came sites in which information was combined with a basic service. By the time of the third generation, websites offered basic personalization, recognizing surfers and their preferences. This was the start of so-called "Permission Advertising," designed to turn strangers into friends and friends into loyal customers.

Among the first businesses to feature this facility was Amazon, which first appeared on the web in 1995. The company didn't make a profit until the first quarter of 2001, when it made $5 million net of all expenses; a year earlier, it had made a loss of $545 million.

The internet, of course, is more than a place to find pictures of people having sex with dogs.
Philip Elmer-Dewitt, *Time* magazine

Tim Berners-Lee's open platform gave surfers of any age unfettered access to material previously available only to consenting adults. Soul traders were offered the equivalent of a direct line into consumers' wallets. That kind of proposition was of particular interest to marketers of pornography, who offered singles and couples, especially men, the chance to upload pictures of themselves as well to independently rate uploaded pictures of women or other men.

Gary Kremen registered the domain Sex.com in 1994. By 1997, internet porn sales were worth over $140 million and that figure was predicted to rise to over to $366 million by 2001. The mantra for the sex industry was "convert perversions into (profitable) conversions." It wasn't uncommon for sites to generate over $3 million a month. In the same year that Mr Kremen had his name placed on the Sex.com domain register, the Playboy website averaged five million hits per day. By November 1998 there were 60,000 sexually explicit sites on the internet in America alone.

The greatest worry about this growth in readily available pornography concerned the effect on children. According to "e-stats" in America, during 1996 there were approximately 3.1 million children online. By 1999 there were 17 million children and young adults aged between 2 and 17 online. In 2004, British Telecom said it was blocking up to 23,000 daily attempts from people trying to access web pages containing child pornography.

The web was so ubiquitous that by 2008 the Nielsen Company estimated that there were 253 million users in China alone, and 223 million American surfers (71 percent of the American population). The most surprising thing about this figure is that at the time only 19 percent of the Chinese population had access to the internet, so the real explosion of numbers is still to come.

In the 1990s, sex sites generated revenues using advertising that placed cookies on PCs. Cookies tracked site preferences so that advertisers could offer more content tailored to the individual surfer. Streams of pop-up windows opened at the start or end of a surfing session that displayed even more advertising. "Dummy links" landing unsuspecting surfers on pay sites were designed with provocative imagery, which encouraged surfers to part with what initially would be only a few dollars. Once the surfer was hooked, reminders would be displayed offering to keep the pornography flowing for just a few dollars more. Some porn sites even introduced a program called hijacking: this logged a surfer off their current service provider, muted modems and then forced computers to redial a premium-rate phone line. In 1996 in America the Communications Decency Act (CDA) made it a criminal offense to send "indecent material by the internet into others' computers," yet loopholes surrounding the US First Amendment challenged the Act.

In 1999, Vivid Entertainment developed a full-body "cybersex suit" costing $170. It featured 36 sensation-delivering sensors delivering five different sensations: tickle, pinprick, vibration, hot, and cold. The combination was meant to mimic a variety of sexual sensations. Australian scientist Dominic Choy was granted a patent to create a computer-controlled life-like sex doll providing users with aural and tactile sensations.

The power of sex and the mind was nothing new to soul traders. In ancient Rome, brothels contained stone slabs for beds that were surrounded by erotic paintings on the walls and ceilings. While prostitutes serviced their clients the patrons imagined themselves in the painted world of the pictures. In this way, although partaking in sexual activity, the prostitute actually played a secondary role to the characters in the paintings. With the web, people could conjure up erotic pictures and movies from the comfort of their sofas. For the first time in history such images of dominance and glamor could displace those of real partners, leaving "the real thing" to be considered at best as photo opportunities to upload and share with other fantasists over the web, at worst as little more than "bad porn." It also gave vent to people's rising urge for recognition as individuals. Compelled to seek attention and acknowledgment, they literally exposed themselves to the world.

With long-term personal relationships becoming increasingly complicated to sustain, people looked for more tantalizing thrills and goals. Celebrities wearing brands offered the perfect solution. Surfers and the general public alike could fantasize about owning all sorts of products, as worn by the good-looking celebrities. Best of all, using credit cards, they could order it all online.

22

The sad princess

Goodbye England's rose,
from a country lost without your soul,
who'll miss the wings of your compassion
more than you'll ever know

Elton John and Bernie Taupin, "Goodbye England's Rose"

Soul traders have long used celebrities to promote brands and causes. While many are talented, many more come from nowhere to emerge as wealthy "it" people whose main talent is just being themselves. All are destined to be scrutinized by the press for any flaws in character, fallouts in love, changes in body mass or self-loathing for what they have become.

A great celebrity has a story to tell, one that strikes a chord with the public who in turn identify an associated sponsored product or service in some way with the ideal it represents. One celebrity eclipsed all others who came before and most who would follow—Princess Diana. She needed neither money nor fame but got it anyway. The media loved her so much that she became the most photographed woman on earth. Yet more than this they loved the image of who she was rather than the person shown in the pictures. Businesses and politicians alike believed that if they could sell the essence of what she represented it would be worth a fortune. Some soul traders did precisely that. You could buy it as a mug or key ring.

Princess Diana was the one celebrity who truly struck a chord with the public. The "People's Princess" defied stuffy convention; she was beautiful and prepared to grace everyone with her company, even AIDS patients. The public couldn't get enough photographs of her; press paparazzi chased Diana wherever she went. On August 31, 1997, the paparazzi pursued her to her death. Trying to avoid their cameras, dazed with alcohol and hyped up by the chase to get away from the hunting photographers, Diana's driver crashed, killing himself, Diana and her lover, Dodi Fayed. News of the crash filtered quickly onto the web and media. Her funeral on September 6 was broadcast and watched by an estimated 2.5 billion people worldwide.

The week following her death, I paid a visit to a floral tribute to Diana given by British people. The grounds of Kensington Palace Gardens, near her official residence, were filled with flowers. The aroma was beautiful. I along with thousands of others read inscriptions on cards. Before long a camera crew from a TV news organization spotted me in silent meditation recollecting Diana's short but significant life. One of the crew gingerly approached me. "Excuse me, sir, I see you are upset about Diana." I nodded. "Would you mind if we interviewed you?" I didn't. "The only thing is that you need to cry for the camera." I explained that I simply couldn't summon up tears on demand. They didn't like my answer so I suggested that if the journalist kicked me in the testicles, I would almost certainly produce the required tears. "Wise guy!" quipped the journalist. The last time I saw the crew they were filming a group of young women who, at a predetermined signal, dutifully produced floods of tears. I learned a lesson that day about the importance of image over substance.

Diana's death was appalling, but the incident with the news crew showed that it created an instant brand—Brand Diana— needing a suitable brand image. That meant big royalties, which most assumed would go to her chosen charities. Within the first six months of her tragic death, Diana memorabilia netted over £100 million worth of business for companies. Brand Diana offered businesses a chance to add a sense of solemnity and authenticity to their products. The Diana Memorial Fund registered an official Diana logo to protect her image and name. The logo featured three important marketing devices:

- Diana's personal signature
- Diana's favourite color—purple

- "Official" endorsement through the caption "Princess of Wales Memorial Fund"

The first product to officially use the Diana logo was Flora margarine. Just as people felt they knew Diana in life, so through the combination of the three powerful marketing logo devices it was intended that they would be drawn closer to her in memory. Diana's good name and memory soon became in danger of being devalued. Tacky T-shirts with legends read: "Born a princess, died a saint, now an angel." Reporting in the trade magazine *Marketing Week*, Mintel revealed that most people (60 percent of a sample of 1,492 adults) felt that companies were "cynically cashing in on public sympathy through cause-related marketing."

Only weeks after her death, newspapers reported that beads allegedly torn from her dresses had been sold as earrings at $1,000 a pair. Tourist shops sold everything from Diana mugs and spoons to Diana medals and plates. In the West African Togo Republic, Diana paraphernalia even included a special edition of stamps selling for the local equivalent of two months' salary. One firm even requested an endorsement of an official Diana colonic irrigation system. An internet-based soul trader set up an online computer game based on Diana's fatal road accident. Players "drove" a Mercedes at high speed whilst being chased by paparazzi on motorbikes. Within a year of Diana's death, Diana's brother, Earl Spencer, supported by her son, Prince William, made strong representations for the Princess of Wales Memorial Committee to be closed down.

Ten years after her death a rock concert billed as "a celebration of the late Diana, Princess of Wales" was held at London's newly re-launched Wembley Stadium. Prince William said, "We wanted to have this big concert on her birthday, full of energy." The official website for the concert featured profiles of charities including the Diana, Princess of Wales Memorial Fund, Centrepoint and the

National AIDS Trust. However, according to reports, charities had to pay for tickets; Great Ormond Street Hospital paid £13,500 for tickets. Doug Wright, part of the official team behind the event, said, "The event is not actually being put on to raise money for charity." Instead, charities were "donated" tickets at the cost of £45 each to raise funds. The National AIDS Trust was offered up to 300 tickets. Some went to staff and supporters. The Royal Marsden cancer hospital bought 250 tickets for £11 each.

The British people are the boss

Tony Blair, British Prime Minister

Just before Diana's death, Prime Minister Tony Blair adapted a slogan first heard in 1967 in a song by the Bonzo Dog Doo-Dah Band. The slogan reappeared in the mid-1990s as a registered trade mark for one of Ben & Jerry's ice creams. Third time round the slogan was meant to rebrand Great Britain as über trendy: "Cool Britannia."

Government spin doctors ensured that the Prime Minister and his colleagues were seen with rock stars and celebrities including the newly formed (in 1994) Spice Girls. Like all branding exercises, "Cool Britannia" needed substance. Things started going wrong when, in a "Brits" pop-music awards ceremony, Cabinet minister John Prescott had a glass of water thrown over his head by a member of the pop group Chumbawamba. The point was that itwasn't enough to talk about being "cool"—it had to be demonstrated. Indeed, on the night of the awards, rather than pay lip service towards being "cool" for the benefit of a well-heeled audience, one pop group, the Verve, preferred to play a free concert for the homeless.

People were growing increasingly despondent about brands and social pledges. They had lost faith. Many escaped to play video games, others to the web. Some started buying self-awareness programs marketed by entrepreneurs like Anthony Robbins, who turned society's craving for identity and purpose into a multi-billion dollar business.

With no commitments, even family life began to crack. Brands accepted that people no longer wanted to conform but to retake personal control over their sense of self-worth. In 1996 Microsoft published the slogan, "Where do you want to go today?" What consumers wore and drove and even whom they slept with helped identify them as individuals. Rather than being just products or services, everything was a cause to be defended and asserted.

HIV tests became 99 percent accurate. When some people discovered that they were HIV positive, they had to accept the illness. Incredibly, the 1 percent of people who later discovered that the test results were wrong—so they were not HIV positive after all—became depressed. The illness had grown to define their values and beliefs.

Consumers were met with a constant stream of TV images. Images of John Prescott being doused in water, warnings of an unseen a "Y2K" computer bug, and the vision of political leaders reneging on promises (like President Clinton, who first denied then admitted to an illicit affair)—all of these served only to widen the perception gap between what authorities promised and what society received. The 1990s also saw the final days of many heroes and heroines, including Edward Bernays, who died in 1995, Freddie Mercury of Queen, who died from AIDS and became a *cause célèbre*, and Kurt Cobain, who shot himself. His short life came to represent a timely brand icon for a generation sick of being undervalued and overlooked.

But, as is the way with the cycle of life, the death of one hero led to the birth of another. Not far into the new millennium, a new kind of brand hero emerged, and his sway for many wasn't just cool but chilling. The moment he left his calling card on a Wednesday morning in September 2001, the whole world stood up and listened.

23

The war on the senses

The WTC was not just an architectural monstrosity . . . If those towers had been destroyed without loss of life, a lot of people would have cheered. Everything wrong with America led to the point where the country built that tower of Babel, which consequently had to be destroyed. And then came the next shock. We had to realize that the people that did this were brilliant.

Norman Mailer, American novelist and journalist

After the attack on New York, now known simply as 9/11, a new era began with a "war on terror" that would have to be fought on two fronts: the combat zone and the media. Governments turned to some of the world's most respected PR and advertising men and women to try to sell a conflict that would last longer than World War II. It was a conflict that left the world splintered by pockets of celebrity-seeking mercenary resistance fighters, rather than divided by clear national borders.

As with so many previous world conflicts, while the people being sent to the battlefront were courageous lions, many advisers left in secure offices to guide operations, including propaganda strategies, proved to be lambs. It was necessary to rebrand the realities of war for the internet and TV generation. Over 4,500 coalition military deaths and over 90,000 civilian deaths from violence were packaged as casualties in the war on terror, a sort of nightly soap series featuring the battles between two cantankerous families of good and bad. The media loved it. But as with any long-term reality show, the public eventually grew tired of the format.

———

Anyone who was over 12 years old back in 1963 can still remember where they were when President Kennedy was assassinated. Likewise, anyone in their teens on December 9, 1980 can remember where they were when John Lennon was assassinated. On the morning of September 11, 2001 I was in my office listening with increasing incredulity to radio reports and simultaneously surfing the BBC's website trying to find out what was actually going on 3,500 miles away in downtown Manhattan. I was sickened. Even now, I remain dumbfounded by the audacity of the terrorist attack. No one can overestimate the devastation on families from the tragic loss of the 2,974 innocent people who died in the attacks, including those missing and presumed dead.

Yet, shocking as the event was, perhaps the most revealing consequence of the catastrophe and those to follow, such as the war casualties in Iraq and Afghanistan as well as the bombings in European cities, was a revolting email that I received just 57 minutes after the 9/11 attacks were first reported. The email read:

RE - Trade Towers:
Did you hear the one about American Airlines' new deal?
They'll fly you straight from the airport to the office.

"Knock-knock!"
"Who's there?"
"Knock-knock!"
"Knock-knock who?"
"Knock-knock . . . knocked all your towers down!"

The email typified the most appalling social repercussion of the attacks: cynicism. As the years passed and terror attacks in general grew more frequent, reported deaths in places like Baghdad came to be little more than just another bad news story. I remember being in London during the publicized "one-minute" silence held a year after the atrocity to commemorate the victims of the towers. As I stopped to stand quietly near Tower Bridge, most office workers simply walked on by, eyes front—getting on with the everyday business of their lives. Subsequent suicide bombings in Madrid and London, Bangkok, Jerusalem and many other cities served to sear the concern many people felt; fatigued by the media coverage, some people were left feeling resigned, indifferent and distrustful.

On the morning of September 11 George W. Bush listened closely to children from the Emma E. Booker Elementary School in Sarasota, Florida, reading from *Mastery II, Storybook 1* by Siegfried

Engelmann and Elaine Bruner. They turned to page 153—"The Pet Goat." The President was clearly impressed. He had no reason whatsoever to suspect that two aircraft were on course to collide with the World Trade Center. Neither the CIA nor the FBI had suggested the slightest rumor of an attack. Even after an aide whispered into the President's ear what had happened, George W. Bush continued to listen for seven whole minutes to the tales about the pet goat.

A short time later a reporter asked Bush, "Mr President, are you aware of the reports of the plane crash in New York? Is there anything . . ." Perhaps not wishing to upset the children or perhaps because he wanted more details from his official sources, Bush interrupted the reporter with, "I'll talk about it later." Recalling the day, Karen Hughes, a senior counsellor to the President, told MSNBC, "Once the Secret Service thought they had another threat and tried to get the President to leave, the President insisted that he wasn't leaving. I'll never forget, he said, 'In fact, I'm hungry. I want a hamburger'."

While the world watched in horror, George W. Bush ordered a burger. Perhaps it was all too much information for the man to process at once. Perhaps he didn't want to spark a panic. Or perhaps the world's most powerful man felt that as the world's most powerful secret service team had never mentioned any concrete plans for such an imminent deadly assault the story would turn out to be nothing. Two months after the towers were destroyed President Bush advised the American people to go shopping.

On May 2, 2003, a suitable American-led military response was delivered. George W. Bush stepped out of a Navy S-3B Viking onto the decks of the USS *Abraham Lincoln*. He was the first sitting president to make such an entrance onto such a vessel. Taking the podium, which stood beneath a sign that read: "Mission Accomplished," Bush announced that while the war on terror was ongoing, there was now an end to major military combat operations in Iraq: "In the Battle of Iraq, the United States and our allies have prevailed." The people cheered but history wasn't listening, and the boy from Connecticut, along with a private army of soul-trading spin doctors, was forced to set about rephrasing, rehashing and retracting.

It was becoming widely accepted that al-Qaeda was leaving some members of society feeling deeply sceptical, not just towards politicians and terrorists but towards religion, corporations, environmentalists—in fact any entity selling a cause created for the professed good of mankind. For its part the West pulled out all the stops to sell the consequent intervention in Iraq to the world.

We are all faced with a series of great opportunities brilliantly disguised as impossible situations

Charles R. "Chuck" Swindoll, evangelical pastor and author

Thad Anderson, a New York City law student, acquired some notes from Stephen Cambone describing how, within hours of the twin towers collapsing, his employer, Secretary of Defense Donald Rumsfeld, decided that the attack could be an opportunity to seek revenge not just on the terrorists but on a much broader enemy, including the now uncontrollable Saddam Hussein.[13]

Once the Coalition toppled Saddam it was strategically essential for key countries to welcome the Coalition's occupation of countries such as Afghanistan. In 2006, Hill & Knowlton, the subsidiary of British-owned WPP Group, were paid $4 million to convince the Afghans to stop growing the opium that funded Taliban forces. Hill & Knowlton was instructed to work with a new and American-approved "independent" Afghan government to push appropriate messages to the media.[14]

During the highly publicized war on terror, the ongoing demonization of Iraqi troops saw Laurie Fitz-Pegado, a former Hill & Knowlton employee, publicize a book about the rescue of an American female soldier serving in Iraq—Jessica Dawn

Lynch. According to the publicity, Private Lynch was wounded and physically abused by her captors. American commandos heroically rescued her from an Iraqi hospital and the story captivated the press. However, Lynch later denied the entire tale, accusing the American government of making up the story as part of the Pentagon's propaganda push to manipulate American and global public opinion into accepting and sympathizing with the Iraqi invasion.[15] Testifying before Congress, Lynch claimed she had never fired her weapon as it had jammed, along with all the other weapons systems assigned to her unit. She had also been knocked unconscious when her vehicle crashed and she woke up later in an Iraqi hospital. "They should have found out the facts before they spread the word like wildfire," she said.[16]

Doubts about the existence of weapons of mass destruction (WMD) lingered on throughout the conflict. What was needed was some kind of independent verification of the WMD allegations—preferably from within Iraq itself.

The Iraqi National Congress (INC) was set up in 1992. Their PR was handled by the Rendon Group and, according to the author Solomon Hughes, the corporation was initially financed by the CIA. Led by Ahmed Chalabi, the group was established to stir up the overthrow of Saddam. The *New York Times* reported that in 2000–4 the INC received $27 million in funding. Sourcewatch.com alleged that following Operation Desert Storm the Rendon Group's work included producing videos and radio skits ridiculing Hussein. They also devised a travelling photo exhibit of Iraqi atrocities, and radio scripts calling on Iraqi army officers to defect. Clandestineradio.com reported that the Rendon Group also helped in the "designing and supervising" of the Iraqi Broadcasting Corporation (IBC) and Radio Hurriah, which in January 1992 began broadcasting Iraqi opposition propaganda from an American government transmitter based in Kuwait.

A report in February 1998 by the respected former anchorman of ABC News, Peter Jennings (whom I had the honor of working alongside), cited records that showed the Rendon Group had spent more than $23 million in the first year of its contract with the CIA. ABC confirmed that Rendon came up with the name of the Iraqi National Congress, an opposition coalition of 19 Iraqi and Kurdish organizations, whose main tasks were to "gather information, distribute propaganda and recruit dissidents." ABC also reported that the INC received $12 million of covert CIA funding between 1992 and 1996.

Further media allegations stated that during the Iraq War, the INC circulated stories about Saddam Hussein's link to WMDs (although the Rendon Group denied any direct involvement in this aspect of the INC's remit).

In 2004 the Knight Ridder news agency acquired a letter from the INC to the United States Senate Committee on Appropriations justifying payment of millions of dollars received from America. The payment was allegedly for an information-collection program involving 108 articles in the British and American press, stirred by INC material. Thanks to the INC's "independence," many of the unsubstantiated stories received worldwide media coverage.[17]

Such stories included an article published in the *Sunday Times* on March, 17 2002 headlined, "Saddam's Arsenal Revealed," which told of Adnan al-Haideri, an Iraqi civil engineer, who claimed to have been involved with bio-warfare labs. A *Times* article on November 9, 2001 maintained that Saddam had terror training camps to teach hijacking techniques—suggesting by implication that Saddam was involved with 9/11. As they had not been distributed directly by any Coalition government, these stories appeared credible.

See, in my line of work, you got to keep repeating
things over and over and over again for the truth to
sink in, to kind of catapult the propaganda

George W. Bush, American President

While the demonization of an enemy was relatively easy during the Cold War, by the early twenty-first century globalization meant that enemies previously fought in faraway corners of the earth had agents and supporters everywhere—although many of them were totally innocent of any criminal wrongdoing.

Misguided hatred of, or at the very least deeply-held reservations about, Muslims became a national pastime in many countries. Some Muslims from Eastern Europe had experienced more than enough hatred in recent conflicts, such as those in Bosnia and Serbia that saw men, women and children slaughtered because of their nationality or ethnicity. With its sights set on possible oil deals once the Iraq War was settled, the last thing the West needed was to create friction among its multicultural citizens.

Enter a Texan woman renowned for selling rice, ready to change opinions and perceptions. Charlotte Beers was the consummate career advertising woman. Smart, savvy and sexy, she made her mark advertising products like Uncle Ben's rice. She was the first female vice president of JWT advertising, as well as CEO of Tatham-Laird & Kudner and CEO of Ogilvy & Mather. In 1997, *Fortune* magazine featured her as one of the most powerful women in America.

Between October 2001 and March 2003, Beers served as Under-Secretary of State for Public Diplomacy for the Bush administration. On December 18, 2002, she pitched the National Press Club in Washington a marketing solution to handling America's image with Muslims.

"Here's the way we seek to open doors. You have to have a relevant issue. Anyone in marketing knows that they won't listen unless you are talking in their terms. It has to be someone I can relate to. Let's try to make it as believable in the world of great cynicism. How can we get something very authentic in the way of a third party? We went to the Council on American Muslims to co-sponsor, co-partner this with us. The best time would be Ramadan because it is a time of great TV and reading and thoughtfulness and we have a message about it. Finally we must talk to the mainstream. We really have to get beyond the rather stratified conversation we have with elites and government people (though that's our first order of communication) and get to the people who've been told every day their definition of who we are.

In order to get to these people, we only have one choice in the world of the Middle East and Southeast. We have to buy the media ourselves. And that's a problem because anything that causes paid media is more likely to be propaganda. But we have a means of reaching millions of people not just 200 in a conference who have been willing to come to, say, the embassy.

Here is what we call a collage—a summary of advertising messages. I used the 'a' word. I shouldn't have done that! I mean a summary of messages prepared for the communication into the country about Muslim life in America. When we tested these in Cairo and Jakarta, they came back and said, 'Please don't make them so short. And don't make it all religion. Tell me how it is for our people in the United States with other people.' And this is a view of four of them. We actually produced five."[18]

At this point a video clip was shown of an advertising campaign called "Shared Values." In it an American Muslim teacher talked about students having no problem with her hijab. Other series of press adverts were shown with the headline, "A story of Muslim life in America." Each advert featured an American Muslim giving messages like "The values I was taught as a child in Bandung are the values they teach here in America." Or Abdul Raouf Hammada, a baker from, Toledo, Ohio, saying, "Religious freedom is something very important. Muslims are free to practice their faith in totality."

Whilst the "feel-good" factor showing people sharing a common interest in wholesome American family values may have been fine for selling packets of rice, it totally failed to address what Beers herself referred to as "the world of great cynicism." Most regional media such as TV stations simply refused to carry the commercials. The entire campaign was a disaster.

We cannot allow the multiplicity of possibilities to drag us into complexity

Kevin Roberts, CEO, Saatchi & Saatchi

What Beers couldn't achieve, the charismatic Kevin Roberts, CEO Worldwide of Saatchi & Saatchi, believed he could. His suggestion was simple: come up with a good catchphrase. On March 9, 2005, Roberts introduced his agency to a conference of various Defense Intelligence Agencies. The title of his presentation was "Loyal Beyond Reason." Roberts explained that Saatchi & Saatchi was the all-American agency, representing corporations like Toyota, GM, Ford and Chrysler. His qualifications included living in the Middle East as a senior executive for Procter & Gamble and CEO for PepsiCo, where he worked on Project Babylon to build seven plants in Iraq. Having established his credentials, Roberts delivered a poignant speech in which he attacked Beers:

"TV is the greatest selling mechanism ever invented because it combines SIght, SOund and MOtion. We call this Sisomo. Sisomo has a guaranteed emotional outcome. Sisomo allows us to feel meaning. Sisomo is the playground of the mind. Sisomo is a medium for the senses. When does anyone ever watch TV with rationality in high gear?

You know that Sisomo has exploded beyond TV. The web, email, cellphones, PDAs, DVDs, ATMs, iPods, outdoor video screens . . . The screen has become the campfire of the twenty-first century. The screen is universal and ubiquitous. Unfortunately for the war on terror, America is being out-Sisomo-ed. Broadcasts of bombings, beatings and beheadings, not to mention Bin Laden, are the order of the day. The terrorists have got better pictures, and the whole world is watching. Images of orderly lines at elections in Afghanistan and Iraq have a short shelf life for the daily appetite of the screen. America is at risk of being held as an emotional prisoner in the face of a thousand blogs and vlogs (video blogs).

How do you "Sisomo-back"? What are your channels? And more especially, what is your content? It's certainly not version 0.2 of Charlotte Beers, who tried to repackage Uncle Sam the same way she did Uncle Ben's. Programs about happy Muslims assimilated into America just won't cut it.

We had a brief glimpse of the possibilities with the Tsunami—American helicopters and aid workers in the flow of rescue work, but in many ways the Tsunami was a great lost opportunity. America faltered. It reacted too slowly. My vision of the 'Fight for a Better World' is a parallel track to the war on terror. American security needs a threatening, punitive, brutal and unilateral fighting force full of young, slightly pissed-off males capable of accessing any battlefield in the world. But it also needs a twenty-first-century organization to tackle global AIDS, malnutrition and malaria.

We've got some fantastic programs and organizations on the job but they need more support to achieve faster and more effective results. This becomes your 'product' that you communicate, campaign, recruit for and advertise around the world. It's not enough to reshuffle the deck. You have to start a new game. You have to get people to listen. I have no answer to the culture of death of the suicide bomber. I can't suggest what to do when passion goes bad. But I can tell you that I challenge audiences all over the world that the role of business is to make the world a better place."[19]

Roberts summed up by rebranding the war on terror through a slogan: "A global struggle against violent extremism." Before long American Secretary of Defense Donald Rumsfeld and others were including the new slogan as part of their rhetoric. The only problem was that in Arabic the word for struggle was, in fact, "Jihad." Remarkably, Roberts had convinced America to openly declare their own global Jihad! Once the *faux pas* was discovered, the new slogan was promptly dropped.

I rarely read the stories . . . [I] get briefed by people
who have probably read the news themselves

George W. Bush, American President 2001–2009

Both Bush and Blair began to come to the conclusion that perhaps the best way to control the hearts and minds of radicalized Muslims was not just through advertising but by taking charge of the press itself.

Private contractor Science Applications International Corp. (SAIC), whose vice president from 1993 to 2002 was former

UN weapons inspector David Kay, was given the chance to run the Iraqi Media Network comprising the Al-Iraqiya TV station and *Al-Sabah* newspaper. SAIC had no previous experience of running media empires so it filled broadcasts with traditional Arabic melodies and official Coalition announcements. SAIC's costs escalated from £15 million to £82 million and, as George Packer noted in his book *The Assassins' Gate: America in Iraq*, Tony Blair was hugely disappointed with the tame official media in post-occupation Iraq. "Everyone in Baghdad knew that the media project was a disaster. In London, Tony Blair knew and he was tearing his hair out trying to get it fixed." John Sawyers, formerly British ambassador to Cairo, was appointed as a Special Representative to Iraq with the remit to set up the Iraqi Interim Authority (IIA). To play down the overtly propaganda aspect of broadcasts, he suggested showing daily British soccer matches featuring internationally respected soccer teams like Manchester United and Arsenal. Over the years social soul traders have used sports like soccer to calm social behavior, often offering a welcome distraction from more pressing political issues.

Eventually SAIC was replaced by other private contractors. In 2005 al-Iraqiya started to broadcast a reality show featuring captured terrorists confessing to acts such as drunken gay orgies in mosques. The program, *Terror in the Grip of Justice*, depicted the mujahedin as depraved lunatics. This was compelling viewing for Shiites reeling from relentless sectarian attacks. Many confessors had visible bruising.

Before long, the sectarian war being played off-camera reached new lows with more dead and tortured scattered on the streets. Some argued that it was a prime example of viewers mimicking TV to become celebrities in their own right. If that was the case, not wishing to become pop stars (thanks in part to programs put together by British and American-funded companies), some Iraqis on the extreme right of the political spectrum had set their sights on becoming martyrs. Osama Bin Laden himself couldn't have wished for his followers to have better encouragement.

Scenes of terrorists bombing Coalition forces' trucks leaked beyond Iraq's borders and onto the web, reaching into the homes of impressionable young Muslims. Rather than seeing the footage of terrorists as depicting acts of brutality and murder, some identified criminals in Baghdad, Kabul and Gaza City as heroes acting in defiance against the West and its collaborators.

24

For the love of God and the web

We are in a battle; more than half of this battle is taking place in the battlefield of the media . . . a race for the hearts and minds of our people

Abu Musab al-Zarqawi

Perhaps never before have there been so many despondent people in search of causes to help reinstate belief—if only in themselves. For many the struggle for independence has left them caught in the center of a wrestling bout between self-assertion and institutionalized religion.

In Britain church attendance is lower than ever. In Judaism alone, while pious segments like the Hasidic movement are slowly growing in number, more moderate, so-called "traditional Jewry" is being lost to assimilation: in 1950, European Jewry was 3.5 million; in 2006 it was approximately 1,505,500. Agnosticism is becoming the fastest-growing personal faith in the West. In the wake of all this turmoil there is a gap in the market waiting to be filled. For some fundamentalists this gap is a worldwide opportunity.

In some people's opinion the war on terror relied on young men and women looking for a cause and a reason not just to live but to die. Thanks to the internet, impressionable people could be preached to 24 hours a day. The web remains so potent that it continues to be one of the first weapons of assault used by fundamentalists looking for clicks on sites to be converted to clicks on detonators.

———

Traditionally, terrorists recruiting young sympathizers have conducted their nefarious affairs in venues such as coffee shops, mosques and madrasahs (religious schools). However, these are no longer safe from undercover agencies and whistleblowers, so instead terrorists have turned to the web. Now all they need is the right kind of web channel.

Not all Web 2.0 social networking sites (SNS) have been widely publicized as the "face" to be seen with or "space" to be at.

However, all have the power to spread specific messages to every age, including impressionable young people surfing from the privacy of kitchen, lounge or bedroom laptops. At last terror cells believe they have stumbled on a completely new medium to reach the hearts and, more importantly, mind space of the next generation.

In 2008 the *Washington Post* reported on a former London nightclub bouncer who had become a religious radical. He was Abu Hamza (known as "the Sheikh" to his followers), and he had directed a question to the deputy leader of al-Qaeda regarding the Egyptian secret police: "Are they committing unbelief, and is it permissible to kill them?" Not knowing where to send his letter, he tapped out an email. A few weeks later, his in-box carried a reply from Ayman al-Zawahiri (who at the time of writing has a $25-million bounty on his head). Killing the police was "justified," Zawahiri replied, saying that the Eygptian secret police are "infidels, each and every one of them." Once his email address was out, Zawahiri went on to answer 1,888 web enquiries about al-Qaeda from the public and journalists.

Al-Qaeda is fast becoming "al-Qaeda and Co.," an international network of small yet effective collaborative cells which gathers online. Along with other terrorist organizations, al-Qaeda regularly releases web-based propaganda messages in Arabic as well as English and other European languages. The messages focus on easily marketable, suitably emotive issues such as the wars in Iraq, Afghanistan and Somalia, as well as the struggle for an official Palestinian homeland. Material includes online terrorism encyclopedias, blogs, websites and videoed messages of hate or covertly filmed attacks—all produced with the intention of reaching an international audience of impressionable recruits.

Many of the videos that eventually find their way onto personal iPods are made by al-Qaeda's online media operation, the As-Sahab Institute for Media Production. During 2008, a new video or audio was released by As-Sahab on average every three to four days. In 2007 it released 97 original videos, a sixfold increase from 2005.[20]

Pleading for justice in the court of world opinion

The German philosopher Friedrich Nietzsche once said, "All things are subject to interpretation. Whichever interpretation prevails at a given time is a function of power and not truth." Propaganda is not one-sided. Radicalized Jewish sites on both sides of the political fence either criticize Israel for its heavy-handed actions in Palestine or demand a right-wing orthodox ruling on the land occupied by Jewish settlers. Interestingly, many ultra-orthodox Jews dismiss access to the web as being a trivial diversion from studying the Bible; so when it comes to promoting their cause to religiously like-minded people, many such sites are self-defeating.

But the web has also been used by more level-headed Jewish organizations who understand the power of a slickly-produced, simple, yet provocative message, clearly presented for the internet age.

During the 2008–9 Israeli response to over eight years of bombardment with Kassam missiles by Hamas-led insurgents, an attempt was made to sway biased world opinion against Israel's tactics. One Jewish organization published a particularly powerful video on the web to be distributed as an alternative view to the media headlines.[21] In response, websites such as the otherwise moderate British-based muxlim.com, which claims to be the world's largest Muslim online community, published footage from Iran's President Ahmadinejad.[22] Pro-Palestinian bloggers also published an amateur video purporting to show the aftermath of an Israeli air strike in Gaza. The footage appeared to be full of carnage. The video was picked up by the European TV station France 2. However, it soon emerged that the video was not actually what it claimed. In fact it was the aftermath of an accidental explosion of Hamas' own weaponry at a rally in a militant northern-Gaza refugee camp back in September 2005, an incident that had been reported years earlier by the BBC.[23] France2 was forced to apologize.

From bloggers supporting Israel, a video was shown that purportedly showed Hamas activists murdering guests at a wedding. However, according to a Reuters report of August 11, 2007, the incident was actually Hamas attacking and arresting leading members of the Fatah party attending what Hamas deemed to be an overly noisy party. The *Jerusalem Post* reported on August 13, 2007 that five guests had been detained "for several hours." All in all 20 were injured and four arrested but no one was killed.[24]

> *We can forgive the Arabs for killing our children.*
> *We cannot forgive them for forcing us to kill their*
> *children.*
>
> Golda Meir, former Prime Minister of Israel

At the height of this period of conflict, with horrific pictures of Arab children being maimed and killed as well as Israeli citizens under attack from missiles, web-circulated invitations to media-attracting public rallies were emailed by both sides. In London, on January 10, 2009, Radical Islamic spokesperson Azzam Tamimi incited frenzied crowds with slogans such as "Israel has dug its grave—Zionism has dug its grave." The following day a British Jewry rally, supported by various other religious faiths including Hindus, saw thousands of protestors holding placards reading "Peace for the People of Israel and Gaza." Through sponsored text messages, the attendees raised thousands of pounds to build hospitals in both Gaza and Israel. Meanwhile, Major Avital Leibovich, an Israeli military spokesperson, announced that Israel had decided to upload a video onto YouTube. "The blogoshere and the new media are basically a

war zone (in a battle for world opinion)," she said.[25] And so the game
of propaganda ping-pong continued.

The distinctions separating the social classes are
false; in the last analysis they rest on force
Albert Einstein, *Living Philosophies*

So whom did all this propaganda reach? Mark J. Penn, an adviser
to conglomerates such as BP and Microsoft as well as to Bill Clinton
and Tony Blair, reveals in his book *Microtrends* that a 1980 study
of radical Islamists in Egyptian jails indicated that the typical
terrorist was in his early twenties, came from a rural or small-town
family, was educated in science or engineering and was upwardly
mobile. In 2002, five percent of 129 Hezbollah fighters who had
died in the 1980s and early 1990s were better off than the local
Lebanese population that they came from. Forty-seven percent went
to secondary school whilst only 38 percent of the local population
attended a similar establishment. Between September 2000 and
August 2005, three of the deadliest suicide-bomb attacks against
targets in Israel, Gaza and the West Bank were carried out by
bombers who had, or were pursuing, advanced degrees. One was a
law-school graduate.

Harvard University and RAND Corporation researchers used
data collected by the Israeli Security Agency to review a total of
151 incidents that killed 515 people and injured almost 3,500. The
five most educated bombers all blew themselves up in major Israeli
cities and killed an average of 22.8 people per attack, wounding an
average of 88 people. Bombers in the rest of the sample took the lives
of an average of three people and wounded an average of 25.2.

A 2003 study of suicide bombers in Israel showed that,
contrary to popular perception that suicide bombers came from
poor families and so would be more susceptible to propaganda,
in fact fewer than half were likely to come from impoverished

families. More than half of the suicide bombers had been educated beyond secondary school, compared to less than 15 percent of the Palestinians in the same age group.

According to the right-wing Penn, if radicalized Islamic terrorists in America could peddle their ideas to just one-tenth of one percent of America's population, they could recruit 300,000 "soldiers of terror." If they did a similar job persuading just one percent of the world's one billion Muslims to take up violence they would amass 10 million terrorists, outnumbering the American Army by ten to one (based on Army National Guard and US Army Reserve figures August 2007).

Instead of asking them to watch, to listen, to play, to passively consume, the race is on to get them to create, to produce and to participate
Trendwatching.com

It wasn't just al-Qaeda that corrupted admirable Islamic principles; according to Bernard Lewis, a leading Western scholar on Islam and author of *The Crisis of Islam: Holy War and Unholy Terror*, extremist organizations based in Riyadh have over three decades spent £75 billion promoting Wahhabism, which he describes as "the most radical, most violent, most extreme and fanatical version of Islam throughout the world." According to the Channel 4 TV program *Despatches: Undercover Mosque: The Return*, broadcast in Britain during 2008, there is evidence that radicalized Muslim clerics in Britain preach that "when a Kafir [unbeliever, non-Muslim] dies, the whole of humanity is relieved." Videos and books promoting such ideas are quite easily available throughout London.

Al-Aqsa TV, which is run by Hamas, specializes in programs directed at primary-school children. During May 2007, it released a short movie that was available via the internet about a Palestinian schoolgirl longing for her martyred mother. Singing to herself, the girl said: "Mommy, what are you carrying in your arms instead of me?" (The movie showed her mother picking up explosives hidden in her bedroom cabinet.) "A toy or present for me? Mommy, why did you put on your veil? Are you going out, Mommy?" (From her bedroom window, the girl waved farewell to her mother and then joined her younger brother, Ubayah.) "Come back quickly Mommy, I can't sleep without you." (The girl watched the TV news reporting her mother's own suicide bombing.) "Unless you tell me and Ubaydah a bedtime story." (The girl is lifted and caressed by her father.) "My mother! My mother! Instead of me you carried a bomb in your hands." (The mother is seen at a checkpoint manned by Israeli soldiers.) "Only now I know what was more precious than us." (The mother is blown up. The camera cuts to footage of the Al-Aqsa mosque in Jerusalem and then returns to see the girl walking down the stairs of her home.) "My love (for Muhammad) will not be (merely) words. I am following in her footsteps!" (The girl picks up explosives from her mother's bedroom cabinet.) "My mother! My mother!"[26]

It seems that, thanks to the web, the spirit and intellect of independent thinkers and even the very young are being lost. However, what soul traders working in politics, religion as well commerce didn't bank on was the development of a more media-savvy generation, poker-faced and ready to deal a new hand in the old game called marketing.

Me-commerce

By the end of this sentence another 48 babies will have been born in Britain.[27] A person who reached 30 years of age in 2008 will have been exposed to 3,000,000 adverts, including 300,000 TV commercials alone.[28]

Many major industrialized countries now have an ageing demographic structure. There are now more Britons aged over 65 than children aged under 16. Soul traders have had to cast aside long-held beliefs that the majority of prosperous consumers were aged between 25 and 40. It is time for marketing products and services aimed at the 60-pluses—who will need to work longer just to supplement their retirement income.

Globalization has meant that borderless consumers compete for their own little patch of serenity in an increasingly jam-packed planet. Cities heave so greatly under the strain that aimless commuters on crowded trains are learning to recognize each other by odour rather than appearance. The British population looks set to rise to 71.1 million by 2031 and 78.6 million by 2056.[29]

People are fed up, frustrated and desperate for change. People are leaving the Church to find God. In its ceaseless quest to attract congregants back to the Church, advertisements featuring special prayers for commuters have been placed in free newspapers:

"Dear God,
You may know me. Don't you? I'm not just a person on a bus or train. I'm not just another face on CCTV, or just another login name. I'm me, and I have stuff going on. Love-life issues; bills to pay. Egos at work to deal with—an overflowing in-box. So please, give me strength. Guide me to focus on what's really important. And help me make the most of every moment in this new month. Thank You. Amen." (www.backtochurch.co.uk)

25

The oldest emotion—fear

We never know the worth of water till the well is dry

Thomas Fuller, *Gnomologia*, 1732

Fear is older than the Bible, and it is an emotion equally compelling for preachers of all creeds. A neurotic market is perfect for soul traders, as it allows them to offer consumers a "once in a lifetime" opportunity to act: act on the environment . . . save money . . . secure a future . . . At the beginning of the twenty-first century, the environmental issue was so great, in terms of both urgency and propaganda, that marketing created a brand new approach to manage it—The Ninth P of Marketing.

In 2008, rather than go out, people started to stay at home. They endured a global credit crunch caused by banks withholding loans as well as exorbitant oil prices. High costs squeezed wallets dry. With news that melting ice had transformed the North Pole into an island, fear of global warming became a real priority. However, the relentless torrent of messages from corporations promising to be "greener than green" ("green-washing") led to a feeling of resigned irritation.

Marketers added a new "P" to their checklist of issues to be addressed. The eight Ps were: Price, Place, Promotion, Process, Place, Product, Packaging and People. The ninth P of marketing was "Planet," and it held great promise of selling products and services in what had become an extremely difficult financial environment.

In 2008 one of Britain's biggest energy companies, E.On UK, had to scramble their spin doctors at top speed after E.On UK's head of power trading, Mark Owen-Lloyd, was asked how already-high energy prices would be affected by a bitter winter. Owen-Lloyd responded: "It will make more money for us."[30] A spokesman for the company accepted that Owen-Lloyd's comments, made during a seminar organized by Britain's energy regulator Ofgem, were "thoroughly inappropriate."

For CEOs, "going green" offers more than just feel-good platitudes to offset guilt from profits. Marks & Spencer has saved up to £11 million a year by charging customers five pence for their plastic carrier bags (see page 58). Significantly higher prices for raw materials and oil mean that if a corporation has a supply chain, it either "goes green" or goes into the red—with profits gobbled up by fuel bills.

Businesses marketing traditional FMCGs (Fast Moving Consumer Goods) such as washing powder and fabric softener realize that more-concentrated, smaller bottles of detergent mean less petroleum to manufacture bottles. Fewer cardboard boxes holding fewer containers can be loaded on trucks making fewer journeys. It all added up to businesses maintaining their margins, reducing consumption, and even helping suppliers with their costs. Best of all, the savings can be presented both as "Corporate Social Responsibility" programs for the good of communities and as a great deal for the consumers' shrinking wallet.

For marketers the prospect of global warming offers the opportunity to better manage dwindling marketing budgets. Costs can be saved on producing expensive color brochures and glossy laminates, and instead PDFs (Portable Distribution Format) can be whizzed off as email attachments. Interminable supplier meetings can be curtailed. In fact, using such excuses as the need to save paper, protect the environment and shrink carbon footprints, expenditure can be saved on virtually anything from plastic shopping carrier bags to complementary corporate gifts.

Consumers have become accustomed to buying recycled goods as the norm. Politicians have imposed additional taxes (green taxes) with zeal. In their quest for green levies, the British government has even managed to fine householders for incorrectly sorting domestic rubbish—and fine them more than if they had been caught shoplifting. Thanks to an overwhelming fear of the end of the world through inaction over global warming, both consumers and taxpayers are prepared to pay for virtually anything, from increased fares on public transport to "revised" home-delivery charges—even if they do so with a scowl on their face.

There has also been a fear of old Cold War enemies such as Russia rekindling international power play over territorial energy resources. Lack of jobs has pushed fears to the edge. In hot countries water has slowly become the new wine of the well-to-do. Everywhere the super-rich offer goods that can be produced more cheaply than ever. In doing so they grow richer while the rest become poorer. Just to give one example, during 2008 a private-yacht manufacturer told me that while sales of yachts valued at less than $2 million were badly affected by the world recession, sales of yachts worth in excess of $2 million were booming.

Mass-produced brands like Swatch have opened strategically placed stores near high-class outlets like Gucci and Rolex, allowing buyers of the economical Swatch brand to enjoy the feeling of mixing with the rich and famous. Brand counterfeiting, although it has never been a minor enterprise, has become a major industry. In areas such as Central Africa, where the vast majority of consumers cannot afford premium brands, nearly a third of consumer goods are fakes.[31]

Many goods—both genuine and counterfeit—flood into Britain from the world's new emerging economies in Asia and the East. Their lower employment costs and increasingly sophisticated technologies, enabling "Just-In-Time" delivery, mean products can be out in the marketplace within days of being ordered. Even large products like furniture and cars can be delivered more quickly, more cheaply, and, best of all, without compromising on quality.

The balance of power in the marketplace has shifted east, and the voice of Eastern European consumers has grown louder. Globalization means that consumers are at liberty to choose goods and services produced in faraway lands to enjoy at home. From beer to fashion, a small world means a big choice. "Glocalization" has come of age: this term, coined in the 1990s by Akio Morita, founder of the Sony Corporation, refers to the trend of marketing locally in the context of a global village economy.

It's small wonder that China and India are in pole position now to take a bigger slice of the world economic pie, and that they pose a real threat of destabilizing America's reign as the "Emperor" of global marketing.

26

Olympic gold

*May the Olympic Torch pursue its way
through the ages, increasing friendly
understanding among nations, for the good
of a humanity always more enthusiastic,
more courageous and more pure.*

Pierre de Coubertin, founder of the International Olympic
Committee

The Olympics have always been meant to represent fair play on the field, but for soul traders the financial gains to be made from the event were never better demonstrated than during the 2008 Games hosted by China.

———

The 2008 Chinese Games offered the first global opportunity of the twenty-first century to showcase national pride and at the same time to establish international business partnerships. For China it was a much-yearned-for chance to finally cast aside the stigma of being a social pariah (*"baininguochi"*—"100 years of national humiliation"); in 2001 the National People's Congress had even passed a law proclaiming an official "National Humiliation Day."

The 2008 Games were hosted in Beijing, a city choked by the pollution created by industries supplying cheaply produced consumer goods and services to the world. The price tag for the event was $40 billion. The budget was 20 times greater than that of the last American Olympics held in Atlanta 1996 and it was the most expensive sporting party ever.

For the world's greatest athletes, Beijing 2008 was a chance to visit the country where their trainers were made and maybe win a medal. For China it was an opportunity to seal worldwide business deals to help support the country's vast and still-growing population of 1,330,044,605. For Western business it was a great commercial opportunity, and the moment when, rather than just importing from China, they could at last widen their export corridors leading to the world's biggest single market.

One beneficiary of China's spending spree was the Philadelphia-based food services conglomerate Aramak, which won the contract to provide much of the catering for the Games. The order included 70,000 kg of chicken, 800,000 eggs, 936,000 bananas and 3.5 million meals. According to a report in *Business Week*, the company was expected to earn revenues of $13.2 billion for the fiscal year ending September of that year. A restaurant in the Olympic village featured a sign reading "We are proud only to accept Visa here."

Local Chinese sportswear manufacturer and retailer Li Ning arranged for its chairman to light the Olympic flame marking the opening of the Games. In return the share price of the Hong Kong-listed company reportedly shot up to earn around £15 million.

During the worldwide broadcast of the Games, pundits in the West waited for TV channels that they trusted for their unbiased reporting to uncover evidence of Chinese double standards. Meanwhile, the TV stations themselves used the event to attract global sponsors for their coverage.

In America, General Electric (GE), the parent company of NBC, secured exclusive Olympic broadcasting rights. The network averaged 27.7 million viewers a night for its prime-time coverage and the channel smashed its $1-billion advertising revenue target by delivering the biggest TV audience for a non-American Summer Games since Barcelona in 1992. Its industrial divisions sold $700 million of equipment to Olympics venues and other Beijing customers. The company also built a 16,500 square-foot "Imagination Center" displaying new products.

Other electronics companies to benefit from services such as security for the Games included IBM, Honeywell, Siemens, Panasonic, and LG. Twelve companies from a variety of industries acted as worldwide Olympic sponsors for the Games. Others sponsored individual teams or athletes.

Every men's swimming event was won by an athlete wearing the Speedo LZR Racer suit. Once the games were over, Speedo launched mass-market swimwear. Speedo promised American athlete Michael Phelps $1 million if he achieved the "golden eight" number of gold medals. He passed with flying colors. Kellogg also sponsored Phelps. In Great Britain (due to host the event in 2012), visits to sports and fitness websites reached an all-time high. Other sports brands using the Games as an international shop window included Nike, which created a new riding boot for American Olympian Amy Tyron.

Coca-Cola ran a unity-themed marketing campaign featuring Chinese basketball star Yao Ming. He already earned an estimated $15 million a year from endorsements and Reebok offered him a contract through to 2013 worth a reported $100 million. Acknowledging the Chinese appetite for speed on the track, fast-food brand McDonald's ran an advertising campaign with the slogan "*jiu xihuan Zhongguo ying*" (I love it when China wins).

27

Brand me

*He goes by the brand, yet imagines he
goes by the flavor*

Mark Twain, "Concerning Tobacco"

Today soul traders and consumers are convinced that they are equally savvy. Both think they know what it takes to create a brand. Channels of reach have become more intertwined than arms in an orgy of octopuses. Everyone wants to make their mark even it means grabbing a needle and tearing a motto on their skin. Branding has gone back to its original roots and belief has become whatever people want it to be. Empathy between consumers and sellers is no longer expressed in their eyes but through fiber-optic internet cables.

The most popular and essential skill for business people and politicians alike is media training, which teaches the apprentice soul trader how to avoid direct questions regarding ethical behavior. Propaganda has been finely tuned by short, sharp and suitably sincere-sounding soundbites. Momentarily people feel that at last they—and not some vague "them"—are truly in control. And they are, for the moment.

———

University teenagers Chris Barrett and Luke McCabe were smart, fun and savvy. They were shocked by the escalating cost of their college education and all that went with it: wearing "cool" branded accessories like Reebok trainers or having Apple iPod players and the rest of the paraphernalia touted by "Brand America." But Chris and Luke decided to take control of business for themselves by becoming the world's first corporate-sponsored human beings.

Offering to have their bodies tattooed with brand names, the enterprising duo set up Chrisandluke.com, where, in return for sponsorship to finance their education, they offered to become living advertisements. Their first sponsor was First USA bank. Writing on their website, Chris and Luke said:

"While we received many sponsor offers, we felt our number one and best choice was First USA. We were so impressed with the entire company. It was important to us to work with a company who wanted us to be 'Spokes-guys' for a topic that was important to college students. We want to make a little difference in the lives of college students and do something innovative and positive! We are very excited about working with First USA and together we hope to help college students across America learn about the importance of financial responsibility and money management."

In return for the deal, First USA got Chris and Luke to promote credit cards to students on campuses.

Before long a plethora of small companies appeared on the web also offering to broker deals with companies like Apple Computer, PepsiCo, KFC and Gap, who offered ten percent discounts for life to any teenager willing to have their ears tattooed with an official brand logo.

In 1997, *The Times* reported, "Having a designer logo tattooed onto one's ankle or wrist has become the ultimate in chic." People even had animals tattooed—such as Louise the pig, whose body was branded from snout to trotter with Louis Vuitton logos. By 2001 the International Trademark Association noted that the Harley Davidson tattoo had become the most widespread corporate logo tattoo in North America. Before that the Nike swoosh tattoo held the prestigious title. One Nike tattoo consumer proclaimed that he got his Nike swoosh tattoo because "I wanted to be different."

Chris and Luke—unlike Louise—came from a long tradition of tattoo wearers. For thousands of years tattoos helped individuals express kinship to a tribe. A 5,000-year-old body of a tattooed man, nicknamed "Ötzi the Ice Man," wore 57 tattoos on his skin. Siberian mummies dating from around 2,400 years ago showed tattoos believed to reflect a person's status.

Modern tribes, free to wear whatever they like—including tattoos—have set out to become personal brands with their own goals, rather than those espoused by commercial monoliths. For them the web is the perfect venue for sharing aspirations. In 2008 the phenomenon called "crowdsourcing" (a neologism from "outsourcing" jobs) saw the rise of small enterprises asking web surfers for ideas to support business projects. So, for example, a dress designer can post an e-shot asking for designs for a new outfit. The surfer who is judged to offer the best proposal can take a share of the profits.

"Crowdfunding" also became popular. Following in the footsteps of Chris and Luke, in 2008 one student, Max Stephenson, asked 10,000 people to sponsor his education by emailing $2.50 to his PayPal account. In the first two weeks after his e-shot, Stephenson received over 2,000 responses and $5,000 in his PayPal account. Such enterprise encouraged social networking sites like ning.com not just to offer surfers a window on the world, but to open for the world a window on a surfer's personal views.

The search engine Google has become a secularist church welcoming opinion makers, opinion chasers and leaders to preach to a worldwide congregation of over 1,463,632,361.[32] Political leaders such as Barack Obama came to pay homage and sway beliefs at Google-sponsored events and conferences.

The search engine has become so deeply ingrained in our shared social conscience that people instantly filter media messages, taking in only the barest details of a corporate or political promise. In his run for the presidency, Obama made mobile-telecommunication history by sending a text message to 2.9 million Americans announcing that he had picked as his running mate Senator Joe Biden. He also promised that, if elected, he would appoint the nation's first chief technology officer.

But the more the unsolicited cold calls, spam emails and banal advertisements keep coming, the deeper consumers dig in, trying to insulate themselves against the endless storm of messages. Ignoring so much information, the world has lapsed into an attention deficit disorder so severe that advertising copywriters are briefed by brands to reduce marketing messages to the sharpest of points and pithiest of promises. Voice, data and multimedia-enabled cellphones delivering content to users any time and anywhere allow brands to broadcast instantly. Soon web-accessible video and audio clips will become more popular than traditional brochures and direct mail.

In the 1960s, no brand manager at Procter & Gamble ever got fired for recommending a 30-second TV spot. However, by 2009 commercial TV had fractured into hundreds of channels. Micro channels were separated into macro channels. Instead of just flicking through a magazine, people could listen to the magazine's radio broadcast via the web, log onto its homepage, blog its readers, download its podcast and watch its own TV show. Every channel offers soul traders yet another chance to exploit a different format for advertisers to reach consumers' hearts, ears and minds. The result of all this is that, thanks to the proliferation of user-generated collaborative content as well as on-demand programming, by the twenty-first century a brand manager at a big company like Procter & Gamble would be lucky to get a three-second slice of the public's attention, let alone a full-blown 30-second slot.

While some commercial brands initially scratched their heads wondering how best to take full long-term advantage of the new channels featuring user-generated content, others realized that, rather than posing a threat to centralized corporate or even political messages, social networking sites (SNS) offered an unparalleled opportunity to be included in intimate conversations heard throughout the web's global chatter. Just as individuals like Chris, Luke and Max had harnessed the power of the online masses, so business could draw on the same force to shrink product life cycles to months rather than years. Once soul traders openly invited people to become intimately engaged with an organization, the rules of engagement were rewritten to make people feel part of a greater cause rather than just occasional participants.

People had always searched for a stage to voice their sentiments about the establishment. The web was the broadest stage ever built; the perfect platform from where they could be heard and seen all around the planet.

Greater numbers of internet-based users meant bigger profits through online advertising, retailing and sponsorship. Perceptive brands proved they were listening by addressing critics head-on in blogs. Leaders in search of followers adapted subtle humor on YouTube videos, or told simple but powerful stories in virtual worlds. Technology had reached practically every home and workplace in the West. As the equipment evolved, so smaller devices delivering exceptionally vivid sound and vision became the new neon billboards shedding light on old commercial and political messages.

In the never-ending quest to capture attention, websites became macro-measured and -managed, not by overall creative content alone, but by individual paragraphs, sentences and words of content luring surfers to the brand's cyber-heart—the shopping cart. Bloggers became opinion makers, even re-editing and reposting the news and communications originally broadcast by brands. Soul traders had taught them that, given the right exposure and technique, anyone could become someone.

Nobodies became reality-TV celebrities. People were convinced that their time had arrived. It was time to live. Time to grow. Time to renew. Time for joy. Time to set trends. Time to build. Time to develop friendships. Time to explore. Time to trade. Time to de-clutter assumptions built on old political and commercial brand promises. Time to rip up the past. Time to be heard and respected.

The moment had come to fight for rights and promote causes, products or services—even if some believed that the means and tactics used to secure such rights were wrong.

28

The next destination

*When the woman saw that the tree was
good for eating and a delight to the eyes,
and that the tree was desirable as a source
of wisdom, she took of its fruit and ate. She
also gave some to her husband, and he ate.
Then the eyes of both of them were opened...*

Genesis 3:6–7

In the future, the unfolding decades will no doubt reveal new soul-trading techniques. Marketing and political science students alike will be as well versed in cognitive psychology, programming, internet studies, anthropology and creative thinking as they currently are in economics, marketing and political science.

Behaviorally-targeted marketing and the semantic web—which make it possible for the web to recognize and fulfill requests of people and machines accessing the internet—will be as important to soul traders as print and TV were in the twentieth century. Techniques such as neuro-marketing will expose which part of the human brain is most susceptible to certain messages, and soul traders will learn how to stimulate such regions using the minimum of physical intervention whilst achieving maximum effect.

Without marketing or even propaganda, people setting out on life's journey to improve circumstances would, to an extent, be rudderless. As with all power, it isn't the weapon itself but the attitude of the person controlling it that really counts.

When conscientiously managed with a view to genuinely improving rather than impeding progress, business, cultural and political communications can play a vital role in the life of both individuals and society. In doing so, such messages don't simply address immediate needs, but become the basis to inspire and unite, and they may endure longer even than any hand-carved plaque which has been sitting on a mountaintop for thousands of years.

Whatever society dictates those messages should be, no doubt, for a price, a soul trader will always be more than happy to supply the demand.

Endnotes

If you want to explore more about the world of soul traders, including downloading additional resources and notes, visit: www.soultraderstruth.com

1. The Dome: A Message from Tony Blair, February 24, 1998: Launch of the Dome contents, Millennium Dome experience website chap 8 (wwp.millennium-dome.com/experience/pm.htm)
2. *God's Capitalist: Asa Candler of Coca-Cola*, Kathryn W. Kemp, Mercer University Press, 2002. Also, "Asa Candler," *The New Georgia Encyclopedia*, Various contributors, 2002
3. *The Corporation*, Joel Bakan
4. AlterNet (www.alternet.org) and Ob Rag (http://obrag.org)
5. "The Roper Proposal" by Fred Panzer, (F 19720501) (May 1, 1972) Legacy Tobacco Documents Library, University of California
6. "Brand logo recognition by children aged 3 to 6 years. Mickey Mouse and Old Joe the Camel," P. M. Fischer, M. P. Schwartz, J. W. Richards Jr., A. O. Goldstein, & T. H. Rojas, *JAMA* (1991 Dec 11: 266(22):3145–8)
7. Quoted by Forces International, www.forces.org/articles/art-fcan/nazi2.htm
8. BBC News website
9. BBC May 2002
10. The National Security Archive website, Saddam Hussein: More Secret History, compiled by Malcolm Byrne (www.gwu.edu/~nsarchiv/)
11. www.bloomberg.com
12. Media Mayhem website (http://mediamayhem.blogspot.com)
13. www.outragedmoderates.org
14. *Jack O' Dwyer's Newsletter*, May 17, 2006
15. *Guardian*, November 2003, War Propaganda, Michel Chossudovsky, War on Terror, Inc., Solomon Hughes
16. www.youtube.com
17. www.commondreams.org
18. www.state.gov
19. Brandweek (www.brandweek.com)
20. *Washington Post*
21. http://sderot.aish.com/SderotPetitions/15Seconds.php
22. http://tv.muxlim.com/video/VibWDVq_YcJ/President-Ahmadinejad-speaking-on-Gaza-Dec-31-2008-ENG/
23. http://www.dailymotion.com/video/x7xekz_gaza-ralit-tv-vs-tf1france-2-lci-et_news
24. Brendan O'Neil, *First Post*, January 12, 2009
25. www.youtube.com
26. Palestinian Media Watch
27. UK Office of National Statistics
28. BBC
29. UK Government Actuary's Department
30. *Daily Telegraph*, September 2008
31. Uganda National Bureau of Standards
32. www.internetworldstats.com/stats.htm

About the author

Jonathan Gabay has worked in advertising and marketing for approaching thirty years. A popular marketing and brand commentator, he often appears on TV, radio and in the press throughout the world. Jonathan is on the core British faculty of the Chartered Institute of Marketing – the global champion of best marketing practice. A much sought-after public speaker, he has written several bestselling books and runs a brand consultancy: brandforensics.co.uk.

You can learn more about *Soul Traders* by visiting: www.soultraderstruth.com